Natural Social Order, Moses, and Jesus

Norman Wangberg

WestBow
PRESS
A DIVISION OF THOMAS NELSON

WestBow Press books may be ordered through booksellers or by contacting:

WestBow Press
A Division of Thomas Nelson
1663 Liberty Drive
Bloomington, IN 47403
www.westbowpress.com
1-(866) 928-1240

The Scripture quotations contained herein are from the Revised Standard Version of the Bible, copyright 1946, 1952, and 1971 by the Division of Christian Education of the National Council of Churches of Christ in the USA. Used by permission.

ISBN: 978-1-4497-9024-0 (sc)
ISBN: 978-1-4497-9025-7 (hc)
ISBN: 978-1-4497-9023-3 (e)

Library of Congress Control Number: 2013905850

Printed in the United States of America.

WestBow Press rev. date: 04/11/2013

Contents

Introduction

How real is your world? The common view is that mature, intelligent, practical adults live and function in the real world. More accurately, nearly everyone tries to live and function in a world that is, in large part, fictional.

A common example will help to illustrate the point. People already know their national government and the ordered way of life it envisions and enforces are man-made and differ more or less from what other governments envision and enforce. These man-made systems and ways of ordering life originated in different dreams or visions of how various human needs and desires might be served according to preferred values and priorities. Whether envisioned piecemeal, through a compromise of different wishes and dreams, or as complete concepts, resulting visions of social, political, and economic systems are artful creations of the individual or collective human imagination. They are fictional contexts for life. They are fictional worlds.

Efforts to implement and impose these imagined worlds result in more tangible artificialities. They result in laws, institutions, and many kinds of practices and social machineries designed to sell the fiction, appeal to emotions, indoctrinate, and coerce people to conform their thinking and behavior to the spirit of the fictional world. The school of hard knocks teaches fictions and so do other schools. Whether by force or choice, people have adapted their lives to these and other fictional worlds.

Other fictional worlds include idealistic systems. Describing and defining admired principles, values, and standards, and building internally logical systems based on them is how we have been schooled to order our thoughts and compartmentalize and organize life. People know, of course, that ideal worlds do not exist outside of the imagination, yet people continue to think and act in idealistic terms in creating and understanding many of the different systems to which they have oriented their lives. The focus in each case is on a fictional system, a context for ordering thoughts and resulting behavior that has no existence apart from its conceptualization by the human imagination.

People nevertheless treat such fictions as their idea of the real world. Whatever the level of people's awareness that they have adapted their thinking and behavior to such fictional worlds, the fictions have become an integral part of their lives. The foundations for the fictions have become foundations for their ways of life. These worlds and their foundations govern how people orient their lives, reason through issues, form opinions and emotional attachments, and behave in what they assume to be a practical, realistic, and productive way. Perceptions, reasoning, and conclusions are reinforced daily by others who act similarly. People's sense of reality and practical wisdom has been formed largely within the contexts and from the perspectives of fictions.

These types of fictional contexts or worlds tend to serve real needs and useful goals, and that has been their common justification. To continue illustrating with the example of government, there is no reason to debate that some kind of social, economic, and political order is beneficial, even necessary, for human survival. There also is no reason to debate that fictional systems and producing artificial contexts for life have been the common ways people have organized themselves socially, economically, and politically throughout history, however successfully those purposes have been addressed. We may argue which fiction and which implementation does a better job of serving which purposes or whether a new fiction or implementation might do better but, other than that debate, what is the problem?

The root problem is that real-world issue. Fictions may be useful for what they can realistically be expected to offer, but can it be wise to live and function in a fictional world? We certainly don't need to do so. We have an original, natural context for life, the only one that gave birth to life and the only one that is necessary to sustain life. The natural world was neither created by people nor constructed from a narrow focus on human needs, desires, and dreams. Yet, other than by study in the natural sciences, people have continued to focus on and embrace fictional worlds in lieu of the real, original, natural world.

Fictional worlds may conceptually accept and account for nature in some fashion, but the adoption of a fictional context and way of thinking automatically arrogates it over any contrary way that nature would suggest independently of the fiction. The essential natural context of all life is replaced by a fictional one that isn't necessary. Nature is artificially lowered to the status of a mere resource to be consumed, manipulated, and abused as artificial values deem useful to the fiction. Conflicts are resolved, whenever humanly possible, according to the superimposed fictional order and way of thinking. The natural order becomes an inconvenience to the human-created, human-oriented world and way of thinking.

What can a fictional context offer us that is different from the natural context that doesn't also, by reason of that superimposed difference and narrower focus, offer illusions in lieu of truth and prejudices in lieu of understanding? Why should a fictional world be treated as more important and deemed the real world, while the natural world we need to survive is treated as a second-class part, if not merely an optional part, of the world? Isn't it better to try to see and deal with things as they are rather than perceive things as distorted by a fiction and to misjudge accordingly? Are we just ignorant, self-indulgent parasites unable to adapt to and live symbiotically with nature?

The narrower focus and human construction of fictional worlds may make them easier to understand, but does that justify them? Are we justified in adapting our lives and ways of thinking to fictions because they are familiar to us or because others try to impose them on us or because we have already misspent a lifetime living in and trying to adapt to them?

If adapting to the natural world makes more sense—and it will if it doesn't already—how would we do it? Setting aside undue fears that adapting to the natural world may require some impractical, primitive lifestyle, would the effort be intuitive and easy or would it require intelligent understanding and hard work? It would be expected to be easier in practice, but it isn't intuitive or simplistic. We need our best intellect to adapt well. For those who seek any depth of understanding, the effort requires a more disciplined intellectual process than merely dreaming up or comprehending a narrowly focused fiction.

An accurate understanding of how to adapt to nature socially, economically, and otherwise requires that we go back to foundations—this time to real, natural foundations instead of narrowly focused foundations chosen according to some human preference. Accurate understanding of the natural world requires that we set aside fictional worlds and the methods for creating them. We must accept the natural world as it is, undistracted by subjective preferences for a different world. An accurate understanding requires a humble, fact-based, natural worldview exclusive of any arrogant, opinion-based, fictional worldview.

A practical effort to achieve that goal requires an approach to understanding designed for that purpose, an approach like that of the objective discipline of the natural sciences, which is designed to discover and rely on nature's rules and standards as free as practicable from subjectively preferred rules and standards. It is helpful as well to consider whatever the natural sciences have to tell us from their investigations. They can teach us much about nature, and we need to understand nature well in order to adapt to it well.

Nevertheless, the natural sciences are of limited assistance. They don't investigate the question of how we should live or, more specifically, what we can do to adapt our way of life to the natural world. This effort therefore is not a science, although it requires a similar objective discipline.

Rejecting fictional worlds involves an entirely new way of looking at the world and at life, and it may require some effort to do so. The objective discipline, for example, is designed to avoid human-chosen rules or standards, however erudite or passionately advocated they may be. It won't be easy for those who are accustomed to thinking in a subjective, opinionated, emotional way about such topics or for those who were never good at the scientific method in school. Nevertheless, it should be readily comprehensible with due effort.

Rejecting fictional worlds affects the foundations for, reasoning of, and answers to all of the most basic practical issues about how life should be lived. This is, at its most fundamental level, a practical philosophical or religious effort. It is based in foundations that are dictated by nature and its order, the original context of life, and by whatever or whoever created that context. Perhaps the most difficult thing for most people, from atheists to religious zealots, will be to consider and accept that this practical, objective wisdom of adapting to nature was also taught by religious reformers such as Moses and Jesus. That isn't, of course, how people have been accustomed to thinking about these teachers. People haven't thought about them, or about God or gods, in a genuinely practical way.

For now it is sufficient to note that a practical understanding of these teachers and the resulting Bible, or of any set of beliefs founded in a belief in God who created the natural universe, requires a focus on the natural world in lieu of systems or worlds of human creation The natural world is, according to the Bible, the original Word of God. The Bible is a subsequent effort to understand it and our way of life in it—that is, how to live according to the order that God established rather than according to diverging human-created ways of life. That effort requires an objective discipline. The effort is obscured by applications of subjective, fictional ways of understanding. As will be demonstrated, the Bible has an objective natural worldview, not any subjective fictional worldview.

A natural worldview generates a wisdom quite different from a wisdom generated from any fictional world of human creation. The perspective and reasoning from a natural worldview will appear alien and unreasonable to those who only see from their familiar fictional worldviews. The natural world works differently and for different reasons. It has different foundations, a different scope and focus, and it leads to different conclusions.

That difference has led people who have not considered a natural worldview to react to the Bible in two very different ways. The easy response has been to reject biblical teachings outright because the teachings don't seem reasonable or practical when people try to carry them out within the context of their familiar artificial worlds. The observation is correct, but the conclusion isn't. It is true that the teachings don't fit artificial contexts but, all biases aside, the fundamental error is reasoning from and living according to fictions.

The other response, without considering worldview, has been to explain the Bible as well as people can either by trying to reconcile the text to the perspectives of their familiar fictional worldviews or trying to create a new system of understanding that seems to do a better job of explaining the text. More scholarly efforts in the latter respect became biased toward idealistic systems. Idealistic efforts try to identify principles, values, and standards within the biblical text and build internally logical theologies, or system of beliefs, based on them. The result is that subjective systems of human creation have replaced an objective attempt to understand God's creation. Religions *about* Jesus have replaced the religion *of* Jesus. Impractical and often enigmatic human-created belief systems have replaced the practical way of life in God's world under God's order that was the primary focus of both Moses and Jesus.

The idealistic approach has dominated Christian theology for centuries and resulted in a wide range of theological systems, messages, and beliefs which, at best, have only approximated some biblical understanding and, at worst, have produced highly fanciful and absurd messages. A need arose under such circumstances to create an orthodoxy, to put limits on that range of interpretations by demanding certain agreed-upon conclusions or beliefs, formulated into creeds. Those beliefs, however, had also derived in part from, and were flawed in part by, the same subjective process. The foundational issue of worldview was overlooked, and it is still being overlooked.

Modern scholarly attempts to understand the biblical text have tried more diligently to consider, among other things, the literary, historical, and cultural context in which the text was written because the original intent of any language must always be understood within its original context. Worldview is also an essential aspect of that context, yet modern attempts continue to try to fit interpretations into one or another idealistic theological system under an unquestioned erroneous assumption that the biblical worldview is, like the theologian's approach, idealistic.

Today, subjective Christian belief systems and controversies abound. Human opinion rules decisions and determines the countless subjective theological systems or versions of Christianity. All have been more or less Bible based, and all may have involved sincere and studied attempts to understand the text. But there has been a general failure to consider the worldview in which the Bible was written and to which it was addressed.

We need to consider an objective natural worldview that avoids reliance on easily misguided human creativity, emotions, and opinions, an objective natural worldview that tries diligently to understand and live humbly in the natural world God created rather than in systems and worlds of human creation.

CHAPTER 1

Basic Issues

P HILOSOPHERS, RELIGIOUS LEADERS, politicians, and many others have offered visions and versions of wisdom about how the world ought to be, what people should believe, and how they should orient, organize, and order life individually and collectively to cope with the challenges of life.

The particular vision and wisdom that has prevailed at any one place and time may or may not have been the most impressive, intelligent, or beneficial. Ideas may have prevailed because of the personal preferences of the strongest in a physical conflict, because of a compromise between wise and unwise ideas through a democratic process, or because of some other more or less intellectual method of choice. However the process has occurred throughout history all over the earth, different people have inherited different visions of the world and different wisdoms about how life should be lived.

As individuals mature, they adapt to the particular world they have inherited. Their world and the wisdom that surrounds them set the parameters for their way of life: how they look at the world, identify goals and dangers, survive or succeed, and, to a considerable extent, select their personal values, set priorities, and make everyday decisions. The wisdom of people's particular world guides them to choose the kind of people they try to become to fit in that world and work within in its ways. From childhood, people have been students of the world they have inherited. They have invested themselves and their resources in a lifelong struggle to learn and adapt to their inherited world, and they reflect their context with varying degrees of success.

People may think, if they have been successful in their adaptation, that they recognize what it is to be well grounded, understand basic realities, have chosen wisely, have pursued life effectively, and be qualified to give advice to others. Successful adaptation to a way of life may seem to be enough of an achievement, but understanding and coping with such a world without actively questioning whether there may be a more realistic and practical wisdom ignores the most fundamental practical issues. It reduces life to a voluntary ignorance and confinement within a world others have created and imposed.

Questioning our own context and its wisdom nevertheless shouldn't be done only for the sake of being contemptuous or rebellious in an arrogant, directionless freedom from others' choices. The purpose should be to improve life only if it can be done practically and realistically. If all we concluded is that a current way of life isn't as enticing as some other imagined yet less practical way might seem to be, what has been achieved beyond a fantasy, an egotistical mental exercise, and a monumental waste of time?

Anyone settled in and proud of his or her current way of life must prepare to be challenged and, in all likelihood, offended by anything different or new. It is therefore obligatory, as part of advocating any new suggestion, to demonstrate to the honest and open-minded skeptic that it is, in fact, better than any current prevailing ways of life. It is the intent of this work, therefore, to demonstrate to the honest skeptic that what will be advocated here is, in every way, a more practical, realistic, circumspect, sensible, and beneficial way of life.

How then might we propose to search for a better, practical way of life? We might, for example, limit our efforts to revising faulty practices without questioning the underlying wisdom of the way of life. Working within the context of an established dominant system is the easiest, least life changing, least offensive, and most praised way to try to improve life.

Alternatively, we might consider creating our own world and brand of wisdom by replacing the foundations and rationales underlying a prevailing wisdom and way of life with those we think have more merit. That is, after all, how man-made worlds have been created. It is how we have been taught to think about and understand such worlds. We have been taught that the way to improve the world is to choose and champion better foundational ideas, principles, and standards about how people ought to live and reason as well as we can from them.

If we were to advocate the foundations our intuitions or opinions choose, wouldn't our foundation be rather limited, uncritical, and arrogant? It is an easy and tempting way to think. It is easy to be enraptured by our own opinions or rely tactfully on the accepted and insightful opinions of others who are regarded as experts without being so critical as to question them and look beyond them for a more solid set of foundations. It is more difficult, but more compelling, to find and reason from foundations that are more realistic and less debatable than those chosen by anyone's imagination and opinion. However well informed any opinion may seem to be, it is still only an opinion.

If we question everything, including our own and everyone else's noblest opinions, dreams, and sense of truth and justice, and insist that everything we propose to assert as solid and reliable truth has the most solid and reliable foundations, then there is only one ultimate authoritative context on which we can base our assertions of fact and truth: the natural world. The natural world is the only ordered context that exists and works independently of people's imaginations, preferences, and opinions. It is the only world people didn't imagine and create. It is the only world people don't have to defend or support with mere opinion, conjecture, pretense, rote indoctrination, and force.

The natural world and order is the original context for all life. It is the only context that gave birth to life and the only context necessary to sustain life. It is the only context that is inseparable from life, to which all other life forms either adapt or inevitably fail to survive yet, curiously, people seem to think they are exempt from a similar consequence.

People haven't adapted to the ways of nature. They have made and obeyed their own self-serving ways, their own laws and order, according to their own dreams and ambitions. People haven't pursued a natural worldview. They have pursued visions of different, fictional worlds, trying to create their own individually or collectively imagined versions of a world focused on their own narrow scope of agenda.

People have envisioned and promoted views of how they wish the world worked differently to serve certain comforts, conveniences, and ambitions of mankind or some favored subset of mankind. Over time, people have pursued a wide variety of military, political, philosophical, religious, and economic dreams and schemes. One or another of those dreams and schemes are imposed on, and orient and order human life just about anywhere one may go.

As impressive as any of those dreams and schemes and their resulting accomplishments might be, a circumspect consideration of all man-made worlds, laws, and orders requires the simple but fundamental recognition that they are artificial. They exist only because of the means and opportunity for some people to impose them on others and, to an extent, the natural world. That specific recognition should be nothing new or surprising to anyone, yet what has been widely ignored about the consequences is quite troubling.

The substitution of an artificial, fictional world context for a natural world context has caused people to order their lives to the fiction, not only with respect to their daily conduct, but also, more disturbingly, with respect to what has become their conventional way of thinking about the world. They think of their fictional world and its bases, conclusions, and perspectives as a real and essential part of the world, and they orient their lives accordingly.

Treating a fictional world as if it were real and trying to establish it and force it on people and the natural world results in practices that are real enough, of course. Those practices, including institutions and governments as well as the rules and regulations they create and enforce at great penalty, and the teaching of supporting values and perspectives, are highly visible and imposing. Those practices are what people tend to focus on when they refer to the so-called real world to which they feel forced to adapt, and the practices are, of course, designed to coerce conformity. Nevertheless, the theories or reasons underlying any such set of practices, the foundations and conclusions that govern how any such "real world" works, have rested in a man-made worldview, a fictional version of how people individually or collectively think the world ought to be and operate to serve their narrow scope of interests.

People everywhere have matured by adapting to such fictional worlds, but when people look at the world through the narrower focus and scope of a fiction they treat as real, their sense of reality is distorted. Where a fiction replaces reality and narrows the way we think and live, perceptions, however clear, often are under an illusion. Intentions, however well meaning, are often misguided. Actions, however well thought out and well executed, are often miscalculated and tragic. That should concern you. Illusions serve no one well and everyone poorly. The extent to which one illusion is more off base than another isn't worth arguing. The pursuit of any artificial world, any fiction, any illusion, is a mistake.

The ultimate question in any circumspect examination of life is whether people will ever face reality. So far, fictions have dominated, causing inevitable and unnecessary conflict with and injury to the natural world. Any unbiased outsider looking at the pursuit of a fictional world would consider the pursuit to be misguided. According to the commonly expressed opinions of those promoting fictional worlds, however, the prevailing fictional systems, their resulting fictional wisdom, and the efforts to implement and impose them on other people and the natural world have been praised as epic thinking, greatness of purpose, and grandness of vision.

Does forcing people to live according to a fictional worldview and order make the world a better place? Coercion makes oppression real in order to treat a fiction, an illusion as if it were real.

Would widespread appeal of a fictional way of life justify the effort? Is a popular and collective pursuit of a fictional world somehow more rational and defensible than an individual's unwise and deluded, if not insane, choice to live in a fictional world?

Would a comprehensive and impressive internal logic by which an artificial world might be imagined, constructed, and widely practiced justify the effort? The effort is still dissociated from and an abandonment of any rational, practical adaptation to our external natural world. A fictional wisdom is more a flight from any genuine understanding and honest attempt to cope intelligently and circumspectly with the challenges of life.

At what practical costs, in addition to self-deception, do people adapt to the illusions of their self-created, narrowly focused, artificial worlds in lieu of waking up; thinking circumspectly, clearly, and honestly; and adapting to the natural world in a rational way?

Artificial worlds separate humans philosophically, economically, politically, culturally, spiritually, etc., from each other as well as from their natural context of life. They promote all kinds of artificially based disagreements, barriers, and conflicts between people, together with all the related suffering that brings. A natural worldview is the only worldview people could ever willingly have in common because it is objective rather than opinion based.

Internally, artificial law and order is imposed on a captive citizenry by such overwhelming physical, economic, and psychological coercion, including the force of law backed by the full coercive power of the government, that it becomes more practical in that coercive context to obey and conform than not to do so. That coercion is so pervasive in common experience that most people have become numbed to its presence and accept their daily oppression as an essential part of life when it is, instead, the result of an unnecessarily coercive and poorly designed artificial form of civilization.

It may be helpful to illustrate this unnecessary oppression and its source by distinguishing two categories of human suffering. One category is suffering that is a natural part of life. Risks may include, in the broader perspective, aspects of the same great and complex scheme of nature which, despite its individual catastrophes, nevertheless has generated and supported diverse and abundant life over time, creating the natural world that now exists. These risks are an inevitable part of any life, regardless of the practical context chosen. We can learn to cope with and accept them if and when we can't avoid them.

The other category of suffering no one should endure. It isn't part of the natural world, and there is no justification for its existence. It is the all-too-familiar suffering that mankind voluntary and systematically adds to the world.

Rapt in the demands of their particular fiction, people don't seem to take time to look circumspectly, to step back and examine their lives from any perspective other than the illusion dictated by their particular fictional wisdom, much less consider how much more rational it would be to order their lives according to the natural world.

Thinking within the perspective of fictions, people may believe the natural world has little or nothing to do with advancing human civilization, perhaps even thinking of it as counterproductive. Contrary to some people's fears, however, adapting to nature is not opting for a lack of order because nature has its own laws and order. Contrary to some people's fears, adapting to nature will not require living in caves hunting and gathering or perhaps some other simplistic lifestyle to which modern people can no longer practicably adapt.

As will be shown, adapting to nature isn't anti-civilization, anti-science, anti-knowledge, or anti-progress. It is the opposite of these notions. Adapting to nature most fundamentally rejects the illusions created by orienting ourselves to fictional worlds. It rejects efforts that suppress truth, oppress people, and cause things to be misused and abused to elevate a fiction above what is real, pursue the fiction as if it were real, and let what is real suffer the consequences.

Adapting to nature is an effort to live according to its order, supporting the natural world that supports us, instead of mistreating and depleting the natural world to build up a fictional world.

In our collective pursuit of fictional worlds, elevating them over reality, we have thought of ourselves as above and apart from nature and, in many respects, in conflict with nature and each other. Whatever fiction we have arrogated, we have treated nature as if it were something less than us, something beneath us and our grand fictions. We have treated nature contemptuously as something to be conquered and altered at will to fit our fictions. We have measured our success by the extent to which we have used nature as a resource for parasitically funding the pursuit of our fictional world—as if a fiction were more important than the natural world.

We have built up our fictions at the expense of all that is real and necessary to our survival. We have looked with pride at how artificially rich and civilized we have become without seeing how truly impoverished, destructive, and oppressive we have also become.

Are we merely parasites of the natural world, concerned only with our narrow self-interests and man-made worlds or can we live in and according to the natural world instead? Are we so enamored with artificial orders of life that we can never again adapt to the order of nature? Can we live symbiotically with nature and promote life as nature promotes it?

It is important to recognize from the outset that adapting to nature is not equivalent to adapting to some concept of what constitutes human nature. Its focus is neither so narrow as to focus on humans alone nor so indiscriminate as to approve of anything humans might be inclined to do without considering the context in which we live. Nature has its own context for life and its own order to which human life should, in the natural order of things, adapt. We need to react to that external context, not ignore it and expect it to react favorably to whatever we might prefer to do. Thoughts and desires, parading under the arrogant notion that the inner self somehow automatically expresses truth or a correct nature, are a rejection of nature's order and an attempt to live instead in a fictional world of self-centered caprice. A circumspect focus must be on the context of the natural world as the world to which life must realistically adapt.

How then do we begin to adapt to nature? We must begin with understanding. Unlike competing approaches to establishing ways to live, which involve creating an artificial world, adapting to the natural world does not require creating. It requires discovering, understanding, and reacting to a basic reality. Discovery requires an entirely different intellectual process from creating an artificial, fictional world. It requires an honest attempt to understand the natural world as it is and works rather than how we might wish it were different.

To understand the natural world as it is and works, we need to approach understanding in a way designed to serve that purpose. A distinction in approaches to understanding must be made, which will be articulated in the contrasting terms of "objectivity" and "subjectivity," albeit in a way that is not necessarily everyone's usual or familiar understanding of those terms. It is therefore critical to make this distinction clearly.

To understand nature and our adaptation to it—how things in nature are and work and which of our proposed theories of understanding of or adaptation to nature is more reliable—we need to pursue a practical, disciplined process of continual discovery, testing, and revision of understanding where nature's laws and order test the reliability of our proposed theories. Objectivity will refer to the process of testing and judging our understanding of the world and adapting to it against nature's standards. (This process is described in more detail in Appendix A for those who may need more familiarity with the objective method.)

How well that goal of applying natural standards is achieved is reflected ultimately in the relative reliability of our understanding and adaptation. The natural sciences, for example, have shown the practical value of such a disciplined objective process, which has resulted in a progressively increasing accuracy of understanding our natural world and its order. However, the natural sciences aren't the only useful objective disciplines. This book will introduce another in the investigation of a question that the natural sciences don't ask: how people can best adapt to the natural world.

The term objectivity is more appropriately a reference to the process of applying the judgment and standards of nature than to any specific resulting substantive understanding. But a resulting understanding is nevertheless also referred to as objective in the limited and indirect sense that it is, as yet, the most reliable understanding derived by the objective process vis-a-vis any subjective process. It may well be that a completely accurate objective knowledge may never be achieved. Humans did not create or define the natural world, so there should be no expectancy that such an external reality would ever be fully within the grasp of human comprehension and expression, but that should not matter. A more reliable understanding of our natural environment is always of more use to our survival, and that is sufficient enough reason to pursue the objective discipline.

Subjectivity, in contrast, is used herein to refer to the process of applying human-selected standards of judgment to any proposed understanding. When human-selected standards— for example, a set of ideals or a compromise of ideals—are used as the basis to reason and judge any hypothesis, the judgment reflects only how well the tested hypothesis satisfies the individual or collective human imagination represented by those testing standards. That testing process may become a way to understand that individual or collective human imagination or an artificial construct based on that imagination, but that procedure is not designed to understand the natural world which is not the product of human imagination and perspective. Anything less than a full and exclusive deference to nature's standards effectively creates an artificial system of ideas or beliefs, a fictional world dissociated from the natural world.

However internally well-reasoned it may be, any conclusion drawn from a subjective approach is a fiction in whole or part based in a fiction in whole or part. Fictions have some uses, of course, and the point is not to deny their value altogether or criticize those skilled in creating fictions. The point is to be aware of how fictions are proposed to be used. The objection is where a fiction is treated as a world to which people try or are forced to adapt. Fictions, treated as such, are fine, but it isn't wise to live in them or treat them as real.

There have nevertheless been many fictional social, political, economic, and religious systems throughout history to which people have adapted and are currently adapted. They have been invented and designed in subjective thought. Subjective thought is how artificial worlds function. Subjectivity and fictions are so pervasive that most people have come to think only in that opinionated, subjective way in order to address life's issues. The intent here is to demonstrate that we can apply an objective approach that can help to adapt in a practical way to the natural world and its order.

It may be argued in defense of fictions that people sense the world in the first instance in an entirely subjective way. As far as that statement goes, it may be true, but that is not the end of the discussion. There are critical additional steps in the disciplined process of questioning, testing, and applying objective standards in order to judge the reliability of our sense perceptions and proposed understanding and sometimes to suggest more reliable bases and conclusions.

This need for objectivity is not intended to suggest that people adapting to the natural world must always be devoted to and immersed in the objective discipline. The discipline is a tool to discover and understand how to adapt to nature, to understand why this order and not that, but people routinely live ordered daily lives following many other pursuits without need to understand every reason behind every order to their lives or spending every hour on its study.

Analogously, we don't have to be a scientist to use many scientific and technological innovations, but we must be a scientist to understand and develop that science and technology. Because understanding is the purpose here, the focus is on the objective discipline and what it can provide to the core of our understanding and way of life in order to be as realistic as possible. The focus is not intended to diminish the great scope of life but to put it on the most realistic, practical, and rational of all foundations.

The objective process, by applying nature's standards in lieu of human-chosen standards, rests its authority on those objective standards. That is an authority independent of the opinions or reputation of those (including this author) who try to apply the objective process. Where authority is based on subjective opinion, in contrast, the opinion and therefore the reputation, integrity, and reliability of the person offering it are at issue. The proper focus in an objective effort is not on those who apply objective standards because nature's standards don't differ depending on whoever applies them and because one's opinions are merely hypotheses that need to be tested against nature's standards. The wisdom to be deduced doesn't belong to any human imagination or wisdom. It is a wisdom inherent in adapting to the natural world. The focus for authority and criticism is on how well the objective process was executed and on the logic, circumspection, and ultimate reliability of its conclusions. As experience suggests additional testing against nature's standards, building on past efforts, the logic and reliability of understanding improves.

Such is the state of our knowledge. We do the best we can. This book does not claim to contain all the answers. It claims that we need to be realistic and adapt to nature in a practical way, that the objective process is the better way of approaching our understanding of and adaptation to the natural world, and that this effort tries to offer a reasonable initial working understanding on which life can be ordered in a practical way and from which the objective effort may be continued.

CHAPTER 2

Goals

T HIS BOOK HAS two main goals in its attempt to focus on the natural world rather than on fictional worlds. Each goal addresses a different area of study and conventional understanding where decisions are currently dominated by subjectivity, but objectivity ought to dominate. The first goal, as already introduced, relates to the general way in which people order their lives.

The second goal is related to the first, but it needs separate and delicate introduction because of the sensitivities and prejudices that subjective systems of understanding have already produced. It addresses religion but in a different and more practical way than modern people have been accustomed. The purpose is not to offend but to put life and understanding on more solid foundations.

Again, the challenge here is how people perceive the world

and order their practical relation to it. The challenge to reject fictions as the basis for orienting and ordering life is put to everyone, both to the religious and nonreligious.

When we focus on the practical and functional, rather than on the abstract and impractical, how we attempt to live is our applied religion. It is the practical expression of what we genuinely believe is our place and purpose in life as best we understand it. Our attempts may be frustrated by oppressions or misdirected by illusion or trickery, but we still try to rely on our basic understanding. Fundamental belief and resulting behavior are practical religious issues and are obviously affected by fictional vs. natural worldviews.

In this realistic, practical perspective, everyone is religious. Everyone has and is guided by some idea or source regarding how and why they want to order their lives and teach their children to live. Some people may have simply stopped calling their chosen way of life a religion and stopped referring to gods because of some preconceived opinion about what a god is supposed to be. But such a focus overlooks the more basic, practical question of function.

In a practical, functional sense, that which governs your life is your god. A god is whoever or whatever becomes an ultimate judge or determinant of the wisdom of your way of life. Whichever reference is of ultimate importance for the way you order your life is your god. For example, an ultimate resort to principles or ideals functionally makes those principles or ideals your gods. In this practical sense, everyone needs and has a god of some kind, just as they need order and purpose to their lives. The practical focus should be, and will be, on choosing wisely.

A common modern rationale for avoiding talk about gods is the pretense of adhering to science, but that fails to address the practical issue. Religion and the natural sciences ask different questions about the world in which we live. The natural sciences ask basic cause and effect questions about nature and its physical rules, but they don't ask the practical god question. They don't ask what is most important for the purposes of ordering human life to the natural world—or any human-created world for that matter. The god question is outside of their purview of inquiry, so it is absurd to expect science to have anything to say about any god unless the religion claims that such god is somehow directly verifiable scientifically. Otherwise, it is neither scientific nor unscientific to talk about a god any more than it is to prefer democracy to monarchy or one social ethic over another. The separate objective discipline addressed in this book, however, does ask such questions. The practical god question is asked, and it is essential to ask it if there are to be mature, identifiable foundations for the way people order their lives.

Another relatively modern attempt to avoid religious language in addressing what should be recognized as basically a religious issue may be found in modern attempts to separate church from state, religion from social order and behavior. In practice, however, aside from oppression, illusion, or trickery, actions reflect what one believes, and actions are social behavior. Unless our religion is conceptually reduced to beliefs of no substantive practical influence on how life is to be lived, and no known religion does that, religion and state are inevitably in conflict because both address the same issues of how life ought to be lived.

The conflict exists not because different institutions cannot be formally separated but because an individual cannot live faithfully according to two different orders of life at the same time. In Jesus' words, in Matthew 6:24, we cannot serve two masters. The practical religious purpose and the ultimate quest of any so-called nonreligious political purposes ought to be functionally the same: to understand and pursue the best way to order our lives.

As indicated in Chapter 1, the most realistic and practical way to order people's lives is compatibly with the natural world rather than with any imagined context for life. Adapting to the natural world requires an objective, fact-based understanding, and acceptance of the natural world and its underlying order as it is and not how we would want to create the world differently. The god question addresses a god tied to that underlying natural order, whether by identity or causation, as the ultimate reference for the way we order our lives in lieu of any god we might create or define in our imaginations. This god question will be addressed in greater detail later in this book, but such a god should at least begin to sound familiar to Christians, Jews, and Muslims, who already claim to worship God who is the Creator of the natural world.

The second goal of this book, more specifically, is to recognize and begin to demonstrate that Moses and Jesus taught the same honest, objective, practical, and liberating message of ordering life according to the natural order, based on a natural worldview, in opposition to any idealistic or other fictional order or worldview. The basis for this proposition is the message that confronts even the casual reader of the Bible: Biblical teaching concerns the correct way to live in the Creator's world according to the order that the Creator established, free from the illusions of fictional worlds and ways that people have arrogantly created for themselves.

The exodus Moses led was fundamentally about changing to a life under God's order and a freedom from slavery to illusions and oppressions that characterize efforts to force man-made orders, religious or supposedly otherwise, on people and the natural world. As will be demonstrated, Jesus' teaching was a revival of Moses' basic efforts. Their teaching and the resulting Bible operate under a natural worldview.

The common notion that the teachings of Moses or Jesus do not work in the real world is a reversal of the truth. That notion views one or more fictional worlds as the real world and the real natural world as if it weren't real.

Belief in God who is the Creator of the natural world looks to the natural world as the evidence of the Creator's choices about a context for life and makes the natural world the ultimate practical focus for ordering life. As will be shown, the Bible substantially derives its teaching from that understanding. According to the first chapters of the Bible, however creation came about (and the first two chapters, if read closely, note two different theories about the sequence), the resulting order and natural world is the original Word of God. The natural world and its order is the important context for our lives. (See also Appendix B regarding the story of Adam and Eve.)

Focusing on the natural world demands an effort to discover how people best adapt to it, free from superimposing imagined orders and worlds of human creation. It requires an objective approach like that of the natural sciences. It requires, as a practical matter, a humble acceptance of a god we did not create, a god not imagined or defined in any way by us and our imaginations, an invisible, indescribable God of the Bible which, in one way or another, created us and everything else natural. It has everything to do with worldview and how people think in a practical way about their world and their relation to it.

It is illogical for those who claim a belief in God the Creator to adopt a subjective approach to basic religious understanding, such as an idealistic approach, that creates its own imagined, fictional world as a purported basis for understanding. Nevertheless, idealistic approaches have dominated Christian theology for centuries ever since Christianity became dominated by Gentiles. Gentiles were originally polytheistic, and fictional ways of thinking are, in the practical sense, polytheistic ways of thinking. In fictional ways of thinking, people subjectively choose what is most important to their lives, and they subjectively create and define gods and worlds accordingly.

In contrast, a focus objectively on the natural world and its order is, in a practical sense, a monotheistic way of thinking insofar as it rejects the gods, orders, and contexts for life that people try to create. Similarly, any attempt to try to explain the natural world with more than one god effectively requires some definition and distinguishing descriptions of the gods, which is beyond our knowledge from objective discovery and requires a resort to the human subjectivity and creativity. The gods and other beliefs resulting from a subjective approach are, like everything else subjective, in whole or part fictions of the human imagination.

This criticism of subjectivity is nevertheless not a rejection of all types of subjective belief, religious or otherwise. Some subjectivity is inevitable. For example, evaluation of testimony concerning historical events often depends upon credibility of the witness, and credibility involves subjective testing. A focus on God's natural world as the more realistic context for ordering life, however, requires an objective effort and not a subjective effort.

It makes little difference that theologies based in an idealism, for example, have been tested, in a way, against the biblical text from which they purport to be constructed. The testing has ignored worldview and merely assumed that if the original idealistic choices and definitions, in their advocate's subjective opinion, match the words of the text, and if they lead to conclusions which are, in their advocate's subjective opinion, similarly consistent with the text, the idealistic theological system is claimed to be verified by the text.

Testing idealistic theologies remains a highly opinionated, subjective understanding of the text, and there have been many subjective opinions about the text where people have not paid attention to the worldview underlying it. The strength of subjective foundations is limited to the willpower of their adherents to believe those foundations. (Objective foundations, in contrast, exist independently of any personal willpower.) In the subjective process, the text has been treated as the only authority, a veil beyond which no one dares to look.

Christians' and Jews' focus for foundations for a way of life ought to be the same as the Bible's focus: the natural world and order God created. People have failed to look through the veil at the original Word of God, as the Bible refers to God's creation, and employ the objective approach to understanding required of such focus. People have failed to try humbly to discover the order for life that God established. They have tried arrogantly to create man-made, fictional systems as a purported explanations of the Bible.

It is hardly surprising that idealistic theologies typically assert that Christian faith must begin with a leap of faith, just as any other idealism or flight of imagination would. Idealism, in contrast to the objective natural world, doesn't exist except in the subjective imagination. How else could a belief in a world of human invention purport to be justified than by a leap of the imagination?

In contrast to a practical approach based in the natural world God created, subjective idealism has no solid, objective, and practical foundation on which to build a dependable faith.

Such an imaginary foundation is an illusion nonreactive, or at best poorly reactive, to anything other than its own artificial world. It is little wonder that such a subjective and ill-founded idealistic faith often is questioned and doubted in times of crisis. Only the believer's willpower supports a subjective belief. Such a faith should be questioned long before a crisis arises.

The willingness to accept imaginary foundations by a subjective leap of faith is not a solid foundation for anything worthwhile. Its separation from truth and reality ultimately is persuasive only by an appeal to the emotions, arrogance, stubbornness, violence, and all other devices and strategies for imposing human irrationality and the tyranny of illusions on others. Idealistic beliefs have fostered a systematic practice of violence and oppression, if for no other reason than that the practice of a fantasy can be superimposed and forced on the real world only by stubborn and fanatical violence and oppression. It ultimately makes no difference whether the idealism pretends to reject violence. The subjective approach of idealism is inherently alternative to, contemptuous of and, in practice, violent toward the natural world, whether or not idealists acknowledge it.

It becomes easy, for example, to rationalize a wholesale destruction or waste of any human, animal, plant, or other part of creation for the sake of idealistic goals and dreams. When human-created, subjectively chosen ideals are artificially elevated in importance over God's creation, an imaginary world is arrogated over and imposed on the real one, and all manner of evils are loosed on the earth.

A supposed biblical rationale argued by some people to justify their abuse and destruction of God's natural world for their own selfish pursuits is that mankind was given dominion over all living things (Gen. 1:28). However, that text begs the questions of the substance of the dominion given and whether its exercise is wise or foolish.

In context, as a gift from God, it was a kind of dominion God intended in His world in accordance with His wisdom. However, out of context and not considering worldview, idealists freely redefine "dominion" and the "world" in any way they subjectively prefer, and they tell themselves that they are pursuing God's purpose when they are pursuing their own. Their dominion isn't over God's world but over some imagined world they created in contempt for God's world and the real dominion God would have mankind exercise.

Instead of offering a way of life in God's creation according to God's order, which was originally at the heart of the Bible's practical teaching, the prevailing idealistic theologies can promise their adherents no more than the hope of forgiveness for not living that life. Most modern Christians' hope for anything approaching what they understand to be the biblical Christian life has been relegated to hope in a life after death where the Christian, mired in idealism, imagines that the projected environment will better match his or her idealistic pursuit.

That easy, idealistic life after death idea is commonly referred to as "eternal life," but the term eternal life had a very different meaning in the New Testament. Eternal life originally meant the life offered by God now as well as in whatever life after death God may choose to offer. See, for example, Matthew 19:16–17; John 3:36, 5:24, and 17:3; Romans 6:20–23; 1 Timothy 6:12; and 1 John 3:15.

The kingdom of God likewise is not a reference to life after death or to a different life only after some future event. "The kingdom of God is not coming with signs to be observed; nor will they say, 'Lo, here it is!' or 'There!' for behold, the kingdom of God is in the midst of you" (Luke 17:20–21). It is here and now, and it is a matter of seeing the reality of it and becoming a practical part of the world God created and rules—the natural world.

Because idealism always focuses on some imagined world and because life after death is a handy candidate for a world about which people have no experience to test assertions, idealists have found they can talk about life after death and speculate at length without much fear of evidence to contradict them. It also is easy to reconcile most of those beliefs with what the Bible says because it says little about life after death beyond the general contention that God's justice will ultimately prevail.

What about that life after death? What, other than the wishful thinking of subjective idealism, suggests that God would want to make a different world for an afterlife from the one God originally made for life here and now? Consider Genesis 1:31: "And God saw everything that he had made, and behold, it was very good." Would God suddenly be constrained to adopt some human fictional idealistic world in creating life after death or will the next world be God's independent idea as well? If it is God's idea, and there is every reason to believe that it would be, will idealistic humans again be disappointed and dissatisfied with God's creation and look for yet another, second afterworld conforming to their own idealistic imaginations?

The point is that we are obliged to live the life we have been offered in the world we have been offered. All attempts to create a different world and a different life for ourselves are a dissociation from reality and its Creator. It isn't safe to assume that biblical teaching based on God who created the natural world involves, like those idealistic theologies constructed to try to explain it, a subjective approach, fictional worldview, and fictional order. Reason suggests a very different conclusion.

The basic test for orthodox Christianity should not be which set of idealistic beliefs to prefer but a reliance on an objective natural worldview in lieu of any subjective fictional worldviews, including idealistic ones. Replacing the original natural world and its natural order with any fictional world and its order is replacing the real world God created with an artificial world of human creation, with a misleading and mistaken way of life and of thinking that violates God's world and order.

Absent a circumspect reflection like this one, however, people biased for or against the Bible won't think about their fictional world or their subjective wisdom and perspectives as fictional. They won't distinguish a natural worldview from their familiar fictional worldview or believe there is another way to think about things except from the perspective of their familiar fictional worldview. It is easy, for example, to overlook the significance that the term "world" is used in the New Testament in two very different ways. It refers most often, and in a negative sense, to the world (or worlds) that humans have artificially created and violently superimposed on God's natural world and their fellow humans (e.g. John 12:25, 15:18; 1 Cor. 3:19). The term "world" also is used to refer in a positive sense to the natural world God created (e.g., John 3:16, Romans 1:20). (The Bible sometimes refers to these different usages of world in terms of a time element in reference to the hope for the ultimate establishment of God's rule, the natural order, in lieu of the "present evil age," orders based in fictional worldviews. See, for example, Galatians 1:4. This and much more should become clear as an understanding of the natural worldview develops.)

When people consider only their familiar fictional worldview and the subjective approach to understanding that characterizes it, biblical interpretation becomes an effort to reconcile biblical texts to their prevailing artificial worldview, to try to fit the texts into their fictional way of understanding the world in which they live.

The perspectives and conclusions drawn from fictional worldviews and subjective approaches cannot logically be expected to explain those derived from a natural worldview and an objective approach. Biblical teaching, for example, won't seem practical in light of people's political, social, and economic understanding of how their artificial world works (to the same point, see 1 Corinthians 1:18–2:16). It will seem to turn people's fictional world upside down (in the language of Acts 17.6). All bias aside, the error in understanding must be assigned to the fiction.

Working from foundations appropriate to the Bible's context and purpose is critical to its proper understanding. Despite the best of intentions, subjective approaches are designed to create fictional worlds, not to understand the world God created for the purpose of adapting to it. Trying to understand biblical texts according to a subjective approach and fictional worldview is a logical fallacy.

As observed earlier, the practical, objective approach used here will not produce a natural science because it asks different questions about the natural world. However, it views the Bible in a way that is consistent with the natural sciences insofar as both share a natural worldview and an objective approach to understanding it. This is fundamentally different from subjective approaches.

To illustrate, it ordinarily would be unreasonable to suggest that books written two thousand or more years ago will articulate any understanding of the natural world other than the one in place when the book was written. Nevertheless, modern people have insisted otherwise in the Bible's case because of one or more subjective approaches to understanding it. Subjective approaches, in contrast to the objective approach, are founded on a set of assumed ideals or principles that people have chosen to believe without fully demonstrable evidence. They refer to these principles as "statements of faith," on which their way of understanding their religious beliefs is dependent. Statements of faith often concern an opinion about biblical inspiration and authority that, although intuitively appealing, leads to viewing biblical texts in a way that is irreconcilable with modern science. As a result, modern science appears to be an attack on the Bible when it is only a rational, evidentiary rebuttal of a misunderstanding based on one or more unwisely chosen assumptions.

In a broader perspective, the perceived conflict with science lies between objective and subjective approaches to understanding, but humbly accepting and trying to live in God's world as God made it, in lieu of a world of human invention, requires objective understanding rooted in demonstrable truth. As will be demonstrated, the religion of Jesus (how Jesus lived and what Jesus taught), unlike a religion about Jesus (which has been the theological emphasis of much of Christianity), is rooted like the sciences in actual evidence concerning God's natural world and an objective understanding of that natural world, not in subjective, opinionated assumptions.

The foregoing is not intended to deny the utility of all subjective efforts in respect to biblical interpretation. As foundational as a natural worldview and objective approach are to understanding the Bible's basic purpose and perspective, biblical interpretation also has a subjective element. The text is written in human-created language reflecting the author's communicative talents. The subjective standards by which the intent of the communication is best understood, of course, are those of the author and not those of anyone else in a different time, place, culture, etc. That applies to any book, including the Bible.

When modern readers impose their own subjective standards of interpretation on biblical text, it is yet another formula for misinterpretation. An example of this is choosing to read biblical text literally by applying modern usages and definitions of terminology, regardless of whether the author intended the writing to be taken literally and whether the translator made a complete and faithful translation into the same modern definitions and usage. Neither is a foregone conclusion, and neither is appropriate for adopting an assumption or statement of faith in ignorance of a fact that can be investigated and determined.

The effort to understand the subjective standards relevant to the author's original expressions and communicative intent, distinct from the modern reader's subjective standards, can require considerable scholarship concerning, among other things, the ancient language; literary, historical, and cultural context; and other relevant background and circumstances of the author. Such a study is not a purpose of this book, nor is the study and comparison of ancient manuscripts on which modern translations are based. It is the intent herein to defer to and accept the conclusions of biblical scholars dedicated to such background studies and not to debate them except in the specific respect that any scholar's interpretive conclusions may appear to have been formed from a fictional worldview instead of a natural worldview.

Biblical citations in this book, except for the purpose of discussing the substantive content of the text, are cited to show parallel ideas and not, as in subjective approaches, to try to prove the reasoning of the book. Parallel ideas support and help to demonstrate the proposition that the Bible is, at its core, a rational, objective effort to accept and adapt to God's natural world as it is and as it works, free from subjective preferences for something else.

Biblical quotations herein are from the Revised Standard Version (RSV) unless otherwise stated, but that particular translation is not critical to this effort. A working knowledge of the original biblical Greek and Hebrew would be best, of course, but any direct translation can be used, bearing in mind that all translations will reflect, to some extent, a theological bias toward what has become orthodox subjective theology. It is advisable to avoid, if possible, paraphrases of translations, which often recast or stretch the text to fit the modern editor's subjective theology. In any event, do the best you can with what you have.

CHAPTER 3

Steps to Adaptation

A REASONABLE APPROACH FOR developing a practical understanding and adapting a social structure to the natural world is analogous in many respects to the stages of development of a way of adapting to a fictional world. The basic variable is the context to which we are adapting. Secondarily, the natural world as the focus of adaptation requires an objective process of discovery at each stage of the development instead of a subjective process of creation.

Creating a fictional world begins with subjectively chosen concepts and principles describing how people would like the world to be, that is, a fictional worldview. From that, a vision is developed, either in the form of a concept of how people should socially order their lives accordingly or, as in the case of a democracy, in the form of a procedure for people to choose collectively among themselves how they want to order their lives. In either case, the vision is implemented internally by government and laws, and externally by defined physical boundaries, international diplomacy, and military force.

Adapting to nature first begins with the procedure designed to understand the natural world. It is the objective process of discovery analogous to that of the natural sciences. Using that process as best as we can, the initial effort will be to discover a substantive foundation, that is, a natural worldview. A natural worldview is a complete but concise set of statements about our understanding of the natural world and how it works for purposes of adapting life to the natural world. That natural worldview will be recognized as the biblical worldview.

The next stage is to derive a vision of how a community best reacts and adapts to the natural worldview. The vision should also be recognized as Jesus' basic vision and Moses' basic vision.

The next stage is the practical implementation of the world view and vision, putting that knowledge and understanding into daily practice. For convenience, implementation will be divided into internal and external implementation. Internal implementation addresses how to implement the world view and vision among those committed to adapting to the natural world by adopting appropriate laws, institutions, and practices. External implementation addresses issues that arise in interacting with others who have not yet chosen such a way of life. Some ancillary implementation issues also will be addressed.

Before working through these stages, beginning with worldview in the next chapter, it may be helpful to pause and consider how this approach may help to understand one of the most important issues raised in the New Testament: why Jesus disagreed with his fellow Jews about their practice of the Mosaic law. It helps to understand the conflict in a rational, though hardly simplistic, way that stems from two differently reasoned ways of understanding and applying the law. This may be contrasted with Christian idealistic theology, which typically has concluded that Jesus was objecting either to the Mosaic law as such or with efforts to be obedient to it, but it's difficult to reconcile either of those conclusions with the biblical text. Among many examples of New Testament text that could be cited, the following is attributed to Jesus in Matthew 5:17–20:

> Think not that I have come to abolish the law and the prophets; I have come not to abolish them but to fulfill them. For truly, I say to you, till heaven and earth pass away, not an iota, not a dot, will pass from the law until all is accomplished. Whoever then relaxes one of the least of these commandments and teaches men so, shall be called least in the kingdom of heaven, but he who does them and teaches them shall be called great in the kingdom of heaven. For I tell you, unless your righteousness exceeds that of the scribes and Pharisees, you will never enter the kingdom of heaven.

As generally used in this book, the term "law" is used to refer to one of the methods or strategies employed at the implementation stage referred to earlier. The body of Mosaic law as set forth in the Bible, however, also includes an articulation of the natural worldview and vision without distinguishing it clearly from implemental laws. It is nevertheless helpful to make a clear distinction here because implemental laws logically derive from the world view and vision. These are different stages of development, and it is the implemental law where the disagreement arose.

The implemental laws were derived from the natural worldview and vision to guide life accordingly in daily application and practice. The worldview and vision expressed the underlying spirit or purpose of the implemental law. Understanding the underlying natural worldview and vision as the foundation, origin, and purpose for those laws assured that each law accomplished what it was designed to do, was applied in the factual circumstances for which it was designed, and worked logically and consistently with other implemental laws to support and maintain life in God's natural world. The underlying worldview and vision made the implemental laws organic, contextual, and realistic in their application to support and promote life according to the order God created.

A clear understanding of the underlying worldview and vision enabled new implemental laws to emerge to address new situations as they arose in a way that was consistent with, supportive of, and beneficial to the natural order of creation. The underlying worldview and vision provided the context and, along with testing as the critical step of the objective process, the measure by which any proposed implemental laws were to be judged either as good or bad, beneficial or harmful, just or unjust.

But what happens if the underlying worldview or vision is lost or no longer well understood because of extraneous influences or catastrophes? How should the implemental laws as they had developed up to that time be understood or applied? This appears to be the dilemma that Jesus and his fellow Jews faced, and it required one of three potential responses, only two of which we need to give serious consideration.

(The potential response that we don't need to consider

very seriously would have been the extreme act of throwing out the old law and replacing it with an entirely new vision, a new law, and a new way of life. In effect, that would have been a rejection of God the Creator in favor of some other god or gods.)

A response more faithful to the way of life, and therefore also to the same God, is for people to attempt to preserve and follow the laws as they already know them. This entails an intellectual study of the existing set of laws, that is, an understanding and explanation according to a scholarly tradition of interpretation and application of that body of law, which is what occurred within the Jewish religion.

Such a focus on the law, as interpreted by a tradition, may or may not have retained substantial glimpses of the original underlying worldview and vision. But if the entire worldview and vision had been available, there would have been little need either to treat the body of laws as a fixed and final expression of law with which to address new situations or to consult a tradition to aid the law's interpretation and application. The tradition served as a poor substitute for the contextual guidance that the worldview and vision could have supplied. (The existence and necessity for such a tradition, together with the inability to look beyond that previously articulated body of law, therefore support the proposition that the underlying worldview and vision had been lost in whole or in part.)

In practical application, the focus on a tradition of understanding the law generated a further dilemma. Notwithstanding the greatest of efforts to maintain an accurate tradition of interpreting that body of laws, the focus in doing so necessarily shifted away from implementing an underlying natural worldview and vision and toward enforcing a set of previously articulated laws as understood within the context of a tradition of academic opinion. In the process, an objective approach to understanding was replaced by a subjective approach.

Precisely how small or large the consequential everyday practical changes had become by Jesus' time isn't worth debating here. The point is that any change in focus and approach introduces subjective creation and error that tends to work more or less at cross-purposes with the original objective worldview and vision, which were no longer well understood and available to guide the application of the law.

When new situations arose without the underlying worldview and vision to consult, the limited set of previously articulated laws had to be reinterpreted and adapted to address the new situations, whether or not the previously articulated laws were originally intended or well designed to address the specific situation. Over time, new prohibitions built up and around the original set of articulated laws and impinged on, and perhaps suffocated to a degree, the freedoms and benefits originally intended to be preserved by the underlying worldview and vision. Any subjective attempt to adhere strictly to the law and tradition that consequently developed over time—however well intended, intelligently thought out, or well executed the attempt may have been—became more and more at cross-purposes with the original objective worldview and vision.

Although some implemented institutions and features remained under the tradition and the law still served the people to an extent, it fell short of its original design and purpose. The greatest and most sincere efforts to obey the law, as it had come to be understood according to the tradition, missed its original purpose as expressed by the worldview and vision. The vision of how to live in God's natural world, which the implemental law was designed to support, was not being lived even if the law, as it had developed under the tradition, was fully practiced—and in some respects because the traditional understanding was being fully practiced. Note Matthew 15:3–6.

Jesus' response to the dilemma of losing the underlying worldview or vision was independent of the formal scholarly training in the tradition, yet it was more logically sound. Jesus adopted the third alternative response to the dilemma: to restore the original underlying worldview and vision. Jesus saw the implemental law in an entirely different way, as an implementation of a visionary goal that was the original purpose for such a law to exist. See 2 Corinthians 3:15–16: "Yes, to this day whenever Moses is read a veil lies over their minds; but when a man turns to the Lord [or Master] the veil is removed."

The difference is between looking at the Mosaic law as an object and looking at the natural worldview and vision from which that law was derived. The latter looks through the law to the reason for the law to exist. The latter accepts that the objective was to help order life as God intended, as evidenced by the choices God made in creating a natural context for life. Therefore the law must be understood within the context of the natural worldview.

The Jewish scholars of Jesus' day, who were focused on their subjective tradition of understanding the law, did not see this worldview and vision and consequently misunderstood Jesus. They treated Jesus as a troublemaker unlearned in the tradition, as antiestablishment. They first tried to discourage him by arguing against him, but he was remarkably perceptive and difficult to argue against, especially for apparently not being educated in the tradition. See, for example, John 7:15: "The Jews marveled at it, saying, 'How is it that this man has learning, when he has never studied?'"

To those Jews educated in the tradition, Jesus' visionary understanding was different from their scholarly tradition. They didn't know where Jesus was getting his ideas. To the establishment, Jesus seemed to be an uneducated wild card, to use a more modern metaphor. For example, Jesus criticized the failure to appreciate the spirit of the law (Matt. 5:21–22, 27–28; 9:10–13; and 23:29–36) and what was more important about the law (Matt. 23:23–24). He also criticized compromises that had been adopted because of people's stubbornness. See especially Matthew 15:3–9 and 5:43–48.

To the established leadership who believed their tradition to be authoritative, it might have seemed that when Jesus criticized their tradition of understanding he also was speaking against God and Moses, who they believed were the source of their understanding of the law. Defense of that understanding mistakenly suggested a charge of blasphemy against anyone who superficially seemed to oppose or undermine it.

Blasphemy was a rejection of God—effectively a rejection of the law God gave to Moses. Therefore, it was generally thought blasphemous to reject their traditional understanding of the Mosaic law because it was the best understanding of it that they had. It was, after all, the finest of pious scholarly debate and opinion.

Of course, the original visionary understanding was superior to the traditional understanding, but in the absence of the Jewish leaders comprehending that Jesus had such a superior understanding and was teaching it, the charge appeared justified.

Understanding the objective worldview and vision, as opposed to a reliance on tradition, explains the differences between Jesus and his contemporary Jews without unnecessarily imagining and maliciously assigning a stigma of evil intent and condemnation to one side or the other.

Like most conflicts in human history, and especially among those dedicated to the same god, this was one between different understandings, with both sides trying to do what they sincerely believed was reasonable and correct. The source of disagreement was in their respective approaches to their understanding and a failure of those in authority to recognize what Jesus offered. Those in authority were comfortable with their traditional approach, arrogant toward those who lacked such a level of education, and hesitant to risk peers' censorship by considering a new understanding.

Jesus' understanding did not reject God, Moses, or the Mosaic law or introduce a new law. As will be demonstrated, it was a revitalization of the worldview and vision that the Mosaic law was originally intended to support. Restoring the vision of the people ruled by God, a kingdom of God, brought back Moses' natural worldview and the logical vision based on that view. It would allow the Mosaic law to be understood according to its purpose and support life in and according to the world God created.

Because of the worldview and vision, Jesus was able to fulfill the law. He understood it in a way that those holding to a subjective tradition could never hope to understand. Jesus taught the law and the prophets profoundly, with an authority and depth of understanding his highly educated contemporaries who focused on subjective tradition lacked. Anyone who understood the worldview and vision that Jesus taught could therefore live more righteously than the scribes and Pharisees whose devotion to and effort to keep the law was sadly flawed by the lack of a better foundational perspective and understanding.

Jesus' fellow Jews who failed to grasp and appreciate that objective worldview and vision fell short in understanding either Jesus or Moses. Christians today who fail to understand such a worldview and vision, which is discussed in the next two chapters, also fall short in understanding the practical import of biblical teaching.

For example, modern Christians following subjective, idealistic approaches to theology have derived a wide range of misunderstanding of the law. At one extreme, there has been an adoption of a rigid and intolerant application of individual laws, which Jesus strongly criticized. At the opposite extreme, there has been a misinformed relaxation or rejection of the law entirely, which Jesus also rejected, as evident in the above quote from the Matthew 5:17-20.

As critical as the worldview and vision is to understanding Jesus, the prevailing method of trying to re-create a vision through an idealistic approach and sort of reverse engineering technique based on the sayings of Jesus or other selected biblical texts has provided limited success at best. It would have limited success even if reverse engineering were more practically oriented than idealistically oriented.

The reason reverse engineering likely won't succeed is that the relation between any underlying vision and any finite collection of laws, ethics, or teachings generated from it defy accuracy in trying to re-create the vision by logically thinking backwards from the relatively few conclusions handed down to us. A single vision might be expressed in as many individual applications (or laws or teachings) as there is complexity to life.

In addition, entirely different worldviews might produce some remarkably similar-sounding laws or teachings while having very different foundations, purposes, and effects within their respective contexts. Reverse engineering a single, complete vision from a relatively few articulated laws or teachings is like trying to reconstruct a jigsaw puzzle from a small fraction of its pieces with little to aid the process. Reverse engineering might not be impossible, but it has proved to be elusive, uncertain, and debatable.

That uncertainty in the reverse engineering process, together with the largely subjective approach to understanding within modern Christianity, may lead some to bolster their particular perspective with assertions of additional subjective authority. They might maintain, for example, that there is additional "secret" knowledge that they possess and others don't. In support, they might refer to New Testament texts referring to secrets of the kingdom, but that usage stresses a misinterpretation in a couple of ways.

If anything was intentionally kept secret, it was from those who, in their ignorance or immaturity respecting a natural worldview, would likely misunderstand something when taken out of context and would react adversely because of the misunderstanding. For example, except for Paul's letters, most of the New Testament appears to have been written after the emperor Nero initiated the Roman persecution of Christians.

The potential for persecution of those writing or possessing Christian documents presents an interesting topic that might suggest an attempt by an underground Christian counterculture to avoid a premature misunderstanding as much as possible, using language and allusions that only Christians and Jews more familiar with their culture and the Old Testament would likely understand in order to express what might superficially seem offensive to others. That strategy seems to have been adopted in the language of the book of Revelation, like that of the book of Daniel, for example, but other books, even the Gospels, may have engaged in that practice to a more limited degree. Language mysterious to the dominant culture is a typical counterculture survival strategy, but it is not a strategy to keep anything secret from the counterculture itself.

Jesus' teaching was otherwise secret but not necessarily intentionally (see Matt. 10:27) in the sense that mankind generally, in its pursuit of and preoccupation with its own subjective choices and fictional worldviews resulting in various forms of human wisdom, failed to see what was in front of their eyes from the beginning of time. See Romans 1:18–23. Those seeing from a fictional worldview are not prepared to understand from the perspective of a natural worldview and the wisdom of God. See, for example, Matthew 13:13 and 1 Corinthians 2:6–13. The barrier to understanding results from different wisdoms derived from different worldviews and approaches to understanding. That difference is foundational and will be explained in greater detail in the next chapter.

Jesus' vision, like Moses' vision, was not subjective and fanciful. It was a vision soundly reactive to the world God created rather than to any world people have subjectively created. It involves nothing opinionated, nothing to be kept secret from those willing to understand, and nothing that cannot be logically demonstrated. It is understood by following the down-to-earth, rational strategy for adapting to the natural world as described at the beginning of this chapter. The method begins with the basic objective process discussed in Appendix A and the discovery of substantive foundations as discussed in the next chapter.

CHAPTER 4

Substantive Foundations: Natural Worldview

THE OBJECTIVE DISCIPLINE outlined in Appendix A searches for axioms to express a substantive understanding of the natural world and how it works for the purposes of orienting human life to the natural world. The axioms that do so and survive objective testing will set forth a natural worldview and can be recognized also as the biblical worldview.

GOD IS THE CREATOR

The initial question in focusing on the natural context of life is what most demands our attention if we are realistic and practical about living in such a context. There is order in it. Nature has its own basic way of doing things.

The order governs everything natural, including our

physical bodies, our physical life, and all other life. Biologically, we are made by and forced to live within the constraints of this basic underlying natural order. We need this order and what it has produced to survive. Regardless of the extent of our current knowledge of this order, it is a fundamental consideration in orienting human life to its natural context.

Humans cannot change the basic laws of nature. Within science and technology, for example, the better we understand the laws, the better we can predict results and more effectively use them, but we still can't change them laws. Even when people do something as dramatic as converting matter into energy, the process obeys laws inherent in nature.

Of course, everything in nature does not appear to be ordered. Some of our current perception of randomness may result from our own ignorance of any underlying order to it, just as past ignorance and superstitions have been replaced with a more ordered and objective scientific understanding. Other randomness may exist, even if we were to understand the order of the natural world completely.

Any practical understanding of nature's order must obviously try to distinguish those occurrences that are the consequence of order from those that are a result of random coincidence. In that effort, it also must be recognized that randomness might describe either a lack of predictability or a more ordered sort of randomness. The latter may sound like an oxymoron, but it is intended to refer to those circumstances that produce results that cannot be accurately predicted in the specific case, yet they can be predicted in a more general way in respect to their overall number of occurrences in terms of mathematically expressed probability and chance.

Most randomness in nature seems to be predictable in terms of probability and chance. Even if the specific determinants of the relative possibilities are not yet identified to allow for an accurate and verifiable mathematical expression, general experience might suggest and allow for a certain level of correlated or statistical predictability—much like predicting the weather has been until it is fully understood and predictable, if it ever will be.

For purposes of this discussion, any statistical probability or chance reflects an order, whether or not we fully understand the order. The term "randomness" will refer only to a lack of predictability.

To the extent that randomness exists, it is incapable of objective analysis. Randomness, by its definition, defies any proposed hypothesis of a causal connection that can be identified and tested. Randomness does not yield repeated results essential to the consistency element of the objective method. As such, randomness is a natural limitation on our understanding of the world and how it works. Until a verifiable causal connection can be identified, all we can do is observe that something appears random.

For the same reasons, it is contrary to experience to understand how order could be caused by randomness. While randomness may yield a temporary and superficial illusion of order, merely because that appearance is within the scope of random possibilities, randomness continues to produce unpredictable results, while order causes a level of predictability to results. A purely random process doesn't suddenly cease being random without some intervention that replaces randomness with predictability, a cause and effect.

Any suggestion that, beginning with randomness, order could appear on the vast scale of the universe and persist as long as it has existed lacks support or suggestion in experience. We can subjectively imagine it, of course, just as we might subjectively imagine anything else, however real or unreal it may be, but there is no objective basis for the suggestion. There is no evidence or sound reason to believe that randomness, unless constrained to some extent by some order, can produce an identifiable and testable order. Nevertheless, for the sake of argument, let us also consider that possibility.

In any case, there are only two reasonable explanations for the underlying natural order: the order had an unknown cause or the order in some way always has existed. We also can keep an open mind to other suggestions, but until there is reason to consider them, these two alternatives are exclusive.

For most practical purposes of this discipline, either alternative explanation is functionally indistinguishable from the other. For some practical purposes, however, it does make a difference. Despite the logical equality of those two alternative propositions, there is a practical reason for preferring the explanation of an original cause over the view that order always existed. Focus on an original cause opens the mind to possible additional evidence to consider.

Additional evidence might show, for example, that the natural order of things could change. As remote as that possibility may be in light of past experience, recognizing it instead of subjectively closing the mind to it would be essential. Survival might depend on it.

Other additional evidence might show, for example, that such a cause could specially intervene somehow in human history. There has been an abundance of anecdotal evidence regarding the latter proposition, all of which begs objective testing where possible. Again, opening the mind to the possibility offers the greater practical potential for advancement of understanding. For now, however, either proposition will be accepted as functionally equivalent.

Because randomness is a limitation on our knowledge, at least until an order governing it in some way is discovered, the useful knowledge about the world for purposes of adapting to it comes from the order that exists and not from randomness. Our knowledge of that order may change and improve over time, but the order, whatever it may prove to be, must be elemental to and govern any and all objective understanding about the natural context of life. The underlying order, including its limitations by whatever remains random, is axiomatic for purposes of orienting life to that context.

As indicated in Chapter 2, whatever people deem most elementary and important for ordering their lives are their gods. In such a practical perspective, there is no such thing as an intelligent godless or nonreligious person, or a godless society for that matter. Every sense of order or other basis for making practical decisions suggests a god.

That terminology is unique in the context of this discipline. It needs to be distinguished and contrasted to all subjective approaches and artificial contexts for life. In choosing to orient our life according to the basic underlying order of this natural context, we could be said in one respect to be choosing that order or its cause to be our god, just as in the case of choosing artificial contexts. However, there is a more profound reality to this particular choice.

This choice is the only genuinely rational authority on which we must order our own lives in the real world in lieu of chasing after some unreal, artificial world. It is therefore appropriate to refer to that order, or more preferably to the cause of that order, as "God." Unlike all other gods that we might subjectively create in our mind and choose to honor and accept as a basis for artificially ordering life, this God clearly exists apart from our imagination and clearly did something real apart from our own imaginations. We didn't create this order or this God; it objectively created us and everything else that is real. This God is or established the underlying order of nature. It already rules over us without any choice on our part either to recognize its existence or submit to it or order our life accordingly. This God is god of everyone and everything that is real, whether humans objectively recognize or subjectively refuse to recognize and follow this God.

Although it is subjectively conceivable that such a God could act outside of nature, there is no objective evidence that God has ever acted outside of nature, and that includes the testimony of the Bible. Acting outside of our understanding is one thing; acting outside of nature is another. If this God seemed to act outside of nature, we would be obliged to redefine and expand our understanding of the scope of nature whether or not we could understand or explain the event in terms of our current understanding.

This objective Creator God is invisible to us and indescribable by us except indirectly from the objective evidence of what God has done. The objective evidence from which we can know this God, to any extent, includes most fundamentally the evidence of the natural world itself, which came about according to this underlying order and continues to be governed by it.

Objective evidence to consider might also include, as alluded to above, one or more special interventions by God in the course of human history, such as they can be verified by objective testing. However, history is logically a secondary source of this information, if for no other reason than that any attempt at a circumspect interpretation of history as involving a special act of God must itself depend on an initial ability to recognize the activity of God distinctly from some other historical cause, coincidence, or subjective illusion. That recognition must derive from an initial understanding of how to identify God's work, and that has to come from creation and its fundamental order. Any other source would be based in the subjective imagination.

Based on what is most important to orienting life in this discipline and on what can be understood about this natural context of life, the first proposed working axiom can therefore be articulated most succinctly as "God is the Creator." It might be articulated in other ways, but the substantive meaning would remain the same. This expression is succinct yet broad and accurate enough to express a basic starting point for purposes of orienting and ordering life objectively to the order of the natural world or, more preferably, to its cause.

This unembellished, unascertainable, indescribable God which created the universe is the God of the Bible. That limited understanding about God, except from what He has done, and more specifically by the order underlying it all, begins to explain why, for example, the Mosaic law prohibits any suggested images of God produced from the subjective human imagination. This God, unlike all other gods, is not to be understood as a creation of our imaginations, however much we might desire to create a mental or physical picture of Him. To the contrary, we are a creation of God's mind, to use an anthropomorphism (the application of human-like terms to anything that is not human). We didn't make God; He made us. This God isn't made in our pictured idea; we were made in God's pictured idea, or, to put it another way, we were made in the image of God.

The many descriptions and concepts purporting to represent God that have been imagined by idealists, artists, and dreamers are creations of the human imagination. They presume to picture a god imagined and created by people to one extent or another. The picture is of a false god, even if it is intended to refer to the Creator. The true God can only be understood indirectly by what God did, not directly or indirectly by what people do to try to represent Him. God is not subjectively understood and represented by anything created by anyone. God is not anything created.

It is difficult, of course, to refer to this God that is directly invisible and indescribable. How we use language to communicate an indirect objective understanding of this God the creator from creation and how this God thereby relates to us as creatures can, of course, be expressed in many useful literary ways—as long as the imagery is not understood literally so as to create an image of God in our imagination. For example, the Bible often speaks about God in the literary imagery of anthropomorphism. Anthropomorphism allows us to express relationship with familiar analogies.

Common examples of anthropomorphism include references to the breath, voice, mind, or will of God. Examples also include references to God as "Him" or "Father" and to followers as the "children of God." We also may use the latter imagery in modern language in referring to, for example, nature as speaking to us, Mother Nature, or our own individual inanimate inventions and creations as our "children." Deuteronomy 5:1–5, for example, says God spoke face to face with Moses and Israel. Again, this is only anthropomorphism. The imagery emphasizes that Moses was confronted by a God, who was an external objective reality, not something subjectively conceived in and projected by the human mind.

The imagery of the spirit of God is similar anthropomorphic imagery. It is how we would refer to a person's spirit in reference either to what a person strives to do or has already done. The act of creating is described in Genesis 1:2 as "the Spirit of God was moving over the face of the waters." Order was made out of disorder, where waters also is literary imagery for something without clear form or apparent order and, in this case, for chaos or disorder. Again, language of spirit is useful to communicate what God has done and identifies God's spirit with the order of creation in terms people can more readily grasp.

Such imagery is a convenient and effective communication by analogy, simile, or metaphor, but it is no more than that. It is based in limited human experience, inference, and ways of expressing what is otherwise difficult to express but is not intended to describe God literally.

Any suggestion that such imagery describes God literally instead of by metaphor would be illogical and presume to know something beyond human capability. It would likewise violate the spirit of the second commandment, which prohibits creating or maintaining any representative image of God. It is, of course, a dubious proposition that anything in the Bible would have been intended to violate a most basic commandment, and nothing said herein is intended to do so either. (To the extent that the term "God" as the capitalized generic word "god," which is in all other contexts a subjectively defined concept, might thereby also suggest any characteristics or image of God, it is an improper usage.)

The attempt to derive so-called knowledge about God in ways other than indirectly and objectively from the evidence of what He has done also is subjective and imagined. For example, there has been a sort of reasoning that, because God's nature must be different from human nature, we can somehow understand God's nature by looking at human nature and drawing opposing or contrasting conclusions. That dubious rationale suggests, for example, that because humans are finite, weak, and changing, God is therefore infinite, all powerful, omnipresent, omniscient, unchanging, and timeless. Some of the resulting descriptions could coincidentally be true, but none are necessarily true by reason of that argument. The entire argument is nothing more than a specious manipulation of language after beginning with unverifiable subjective assumptions. The argument assumes, for example, that God the Creator is a describable entity who has a knowable nature discoverable by a mere manipulation of a human-created language. Such assumptions are, more accurately, a description of a false god conceived in the human imagination.

More could be said about this axiom, but the foregoing should be sufficient to convey the sense that God is the Creator. The most important focus for orienting life is on the natural world and its underlying order, or more preferably its cause, by which all life exists and survives and by which everything we might objectively understand came to be and is ordered.

GOD IS ONE

Natural order should not be supplemented with any artificial order for the reasons discussed in the first chapter. Conceptually mixing an artificial world with the natural world creates another artificial world. Mixing subjectivity with objectivity results in another subjectivity. Adding to or subtracting from the natural context creates an artificial context. Focusing on the natural context requires rejecting all artificial contexts and, with them, the gods on which they were formed. There is only one god to consider, God the Creator.

The focus on the natural context and its order also naturally raises the question of whether there is more than one order. Much of our common observation and experience about the natural world suggests that the underlying order of creation is uniform and consistent despite the complexity it produces and the limitations on understanding imposed by any randomness. There appears to be a single set of underlying natural laws, however complex their interaction.

There is no readily apparent evidence that there are distinctly different natural orders conflicting with each other at the same time or alternatively, so that, under like circumstances, different natural laws might apply to the same circumstances at different times. There may be theories, of course, but to most of our experience there is not one order that's applied one day and a different order applied the next. The universe seems to remain consistent in respect to a single underlying order governing all life.

If different results occur under seemingly similar circumstances, experience tends to suggest that it is not because the order of things has suddenly changed. It is that the circumstances are somehow different in an important way that went unnoticed, there was only a limited mathematical chance that any one result will occur under the circumstances, or we don't sufficiently understand the order at present. As our understanding has grown, more and more phenomena that were previously inexplicable and unpredictable continue to find explanation and support the view that a single, consistent natural order governs everything. Until multiple orders can explain anything relevant to our adaptation to the natural world better than a single natural order, for example, some type of randomness, there is no reason to consider that there is more than one natural order.

Having said that, and as comforting as a single order may be in our effort to understand the natural world, we don't have to rule out the possibility of multiple orders. If there are two or more natural orders, shouldn't we try to live accordingly for the same reasons already discussed?

If there were multiple natural orders, it would make the natural context more complex and difficult to understand, but the same task is to live in accordance with whatever order (or orders) exists and is pertinent in the circumstances. The fact would remain that, for purposes of this discipline, our singular focus for ordering our lives has to be on the natural order of this natural context of life, whether that naturally occurring order is one or many.

Alternatively, if we were to suggest that several gods were involved in creating the natural world, we would place ourselves in the position of trying to distinguish them, which is still beyond our knowledge. We would have to decide, based on our subjective imaginations, how to describe and define such a system of gods. The reference to one God avoids that trap. It keeps the effort objective rather than subjective, a focus on the real context of creation rather than an imagined context.

It is sufficient to focus on the natural context as the only real context for life, free from artificial contexts and their artificial gods. The axiom that "God is one" expresses that objective focus on that natural context and its order, however complex its may be, without adding to or subtracting from it by subjective human input.

GOD IS GOOD

The question of how best to live in this natural context also involves a value judgment or, perhaps more accurately, two distinct value judgments, each serving their separate purposes. The first value already has been discussed and justified, and is part of the previous axioms. It is valuing practical, objective knowledge about the natural world and how it works instead of valuing a pretense of subjective knowledge projected from the human imagination.

The second value (or set of values), yet to be considered and determined, must describe this substantive natural context for life in an elemental, axiomatic way

We might, for example, test a proposed value of happiness and phrase the question of the best way to live in terms of the happiest way to live. Happiness is a common human goal. In the United States, for example, the Declaration of Independence asserts that the pursuit of happiness is a basic human right.

There are, nevertheless, serious problems with suggesting happiness as a fundamental value for this practical discipline. Happiness can refer, of course, to individual, familial, or perhaps a social or universal human happiness, but none of these variations effectively describes anything about the world as an objective context for life. It describes only a subjective human preference for how we might create the world differently if we tried to do so.

There is no objective reason to believe that the natural world is ordered as it is and works as it does to make humans happy. Although there is much that is pleasing to us in the natural world, there is considerable evidence that the natural world doesn't always make us happy. Dangers, sorrows, struggles to survive, and death all inhere throughout the order of the natural world and suggest that human happiness is not a fundamental character of the natural world. Ample common knowledge suggests that happiness may result from certain aspects of life, but it is not fundamentally descriptive of the full context of life.

Although further argument should not be necessary to refute a contention that happiness is a value inhering axiomatically in the natural world, happiness also would fail as a fundamental value because happiness inherently depends on something else. Humans are happy when they achieve or have a substantial hope or anticipation of achieving something they value. We always have to ask what makes us happy, and the answers to that question vary from person to person.

Happiness also should be avoided as an axiom because, as suggested above, it is one subjective reason people pursue artificial worlds. It is in the hope of achieving happiness that people often prefer a world where everything might possibly go their way either if they do the right things or strive mightily to achieve what they think will make them happy. The pursuit of happiness is a violence toward the way the natural world works, not an explanation of it. Its pursuit is more a problem than a solution.

Other proposed values that similarly focus on and elevate subjective human-oriented desires above the natural world's order are not descriptive of the real context of life. They focus only on a human preference. They cause people to create their imaginary worlds in the pursuit of those desires to the injury of the real world.

Experience suggests a more objective and descriptive value inherent in the natural world. It seems intuitive as well to suggest that the underlying order of the universe or its cause, which generates and maintains life and does so in its variety and abundance, with or without human interference, and often despite human interference, is good.

Good may at first seem to be a subjective value insofar as it benefits human life and may appear to be subjectively motivated. There is certainly a great temptation to proceed to define good subjectively and thereby to convert any objective understanding of what is good into an artifice created by humans to serve their desires. Good and other values typically are defined that way within artificial contexts, but that subjective aim is not the definition of good that is intended here.

Good must instead be accepted as objectively defined by the natural world and how it works, as it is objectively discovered to be and not how we might subjectively prefer it to be. The fact that human life is part of nature and therefore benefits from that good, just like the rest of nature, does not transform that objective value into a subjective one or suggest that a subjective definition of the value is somehow proper.

A proposed third axiom that God is good describes an objective value inherent throughout this natural context of life. Its adoption as an objectively defined value serves to orient human value decisions to the order inherent in the natural context of life.

By adopting an objective definition for good, we also can say that God the Creator has, in essence, defined what is good by the order of creation itself and how it has worked to generate and promote life in all its abundance and diversity. According to this objective understanding of good, something is not defined as good by the process of any human applying some subjective human value standard and judging nature or anything that God has done as good or bad. Instead, good follows the value standard inherent in the natural world. Whatever God has done is good for no reason or explanation other than the fact that God the Creator has done it. See, for example, Genesis 1:31: "And God saw everything that he had made, and behold, it was very good." (See also Appendix B in respect to understanding the stories of Adam and Eve, and Cain and Abel.)

The axiom that God is good in effect adopts God the Creator's objective value standard and perspective, instead of a subjective human value standard, for judging practical choices. The wisdom that results from consistently and exclusively using God's value standard can therefore be referred to as God's wisdom, such as we can know it from the objective evidence of what God has done.

God's wisdom objectively describes the world and how it works, free from anything imaginary, illusory, and deceptive. It is unlike human wisdom that is founded on artificial, human-centered values that attempt to create artificial contexts and illusions in order to pursue those values. God's wisdom, unlike human wisdom, is not a subjective delusion or illusion. It is real, objective truth as best we can know it.

The contrast of God's wisdom with human wisdom is a critical biblical understanding. See, for example, 1 Corinthians 2:6–8: "Yet among the mature we do impart a wisdom, although it is not a wisdom of this age or of the rulers of this age, who are doomed to pass away. But we impart a secret and hidden wisdom of God, which God decreed before the ages [that is, inherent in the order of God's creation] for our glorification. None of the rulers of this age understood this; for if they had, they would not have crucified the Lord of glory."

Recall the question Pontius Pilate put to Jesus in John 18:38: "What is truth?" This question beautifully captures the irony of a person like Pilate enforcing a human wisdom built on a human-created fiction and presuming to judge Jesus by it. Pilate wouldn't know truth if it was in front of him waiting to be perceived.

God's wisdom is perhaps the most important key to understanding the Bible's core message, which is to live in God's creation as He intended. Human wisdom is preoccupied with pursuing a fiction and cannot hope to understand it.

History, language, culture, geography, and other aspects of biblical background also are vital to biblical understanding, of course, and there are historical texts, for example, that do not require an understanding of God's wisdom. But the basic practical background and religious message is written in terms of God's wisdom instead of human wisdom. That is the reasoning of its core message. Indeed, the term the Bible uses to describe the consequences of human wisdom, laboring under an illusion or deception instead of pursuing the wisdom of God, is "sin," a departure from a true relationship with God the Creator, from living according to the context or world God created, from dedication to truth.

The distinction between God's wisdom and human wisdom is real context vs. artificial context, reality vs. subjective delusion. The most basic distinction between the approach advocated here, as well as its understanding of Christianity and other ways of life, is the difference in the basic context in which people choose to live, on which people choose to focus, and from which people derive practical conclusions.

Biblical derogation of human wisdom is not, as some theologians have subjectively construed it, a condemnation or criticism of the human intellect in favor of some other form of human mystical or emotional enlightenment that is more subjective, irrational, and illusory. It is instead a criticism of human subjectivity and illusions in respect to creating artificial worlds deviating from God's created world. God's wisdom requires as much human intellect as we can muster to understand it objectively and pursue it seriously. The Apostle Paul, for example, clearly wanted Christians to be wise according to the spirit of God. Note 1 Corinthians 1:4–3:23 and note the similar language essentially equating the term "wisdom of God" with the "spirit of God" and "spirit of Christ" and also equating human wisdom, or the "wisdom of men," with his use of the term "the flesh," to wit, a wisdom based on subjective, human-centered values or desires.

Because human wisdom and God's wisdom are based in

different contexts and foundations, conclusions derived from God's wisdom may seem alien or foolish to those whose foundations are rooted in subjective human wisdom—unless people engage in a meaningful analysis of foundations. This contrast in wisdom and foolishness, as seen from a superficial analysis, also is a common theme in the New Testament. See, for example, 1 Corinthians 1:18–25 and 2:5–8. It is also why, for example, Jesus instructed his disciples, "Do not give dogs what is holy; and do not throw your pearls before swine, lest they trample them under foot and turn to attack you" (Matt. 7:6).

Pearls here are, of course, pearls of God's wisdom. The warning is not to expect dogs and swine, the Jewish references to the unkosher or Gentiles (not intended in any idealistic pejorative sense), to understand. Without understanding the natural worldview, they will think that the God's wisdom is worthless to them.

Christianity eventually brought God's wisdom to the Gentiles so the proper distinction became no longer one between Jew and Gentile within Christianity (Gal. 3:28). But there remained an important distinction to be made between those who adhered to God's wisdom and those who followed human wisdom. Distinctions therefore were no longer merely along lines of national origin but on the basis of actually following God's wisdom or human wisdom. See 2 Corinthians 5:16: "From now on, therefore, we regard no one from a human point of view; even though we once regarded Christ from a human point of view, we regard him thus no longer."

People who follow human wisdom also include, to a limited extent, those who are new to thinking in terms of God's wisdom. See, for example, Matthew 7:24–27; Romans 1:19–23; 1 Corinthians 1:18–25 and 3:18–19; Titus 3:3; and 1 Peter 2:15. (Dealing with the still immature will be discussed in more detail in the chapter on internal implementation, and relations with those who do not attempt to follow God's wisdom are discussed in more detail in the chapter about external implementation.)

This book will demonstrate that Jesus lived maturely and taught others to live within the natural context of God's created world, according to His wisdom. That, in turn, identifies the spirit of Jesus Christ with the spirit of God. Subsequently, there was in the earliest Christian church only one context, spirit, wisdom: God's. See Ephesians 4:4–5: "There is one body and one Spirit, just as you were called to the one hope that belongs to your call, one Lord, one faith, one baptism, one God and Father of us all, who is above all and through all and in all."

This passage will be better understood later, but for now it is important to emphasize one spirit that is identified with both Jesus Christ and God the Creator because of Jesus' pursuit of God's wisdom. It is the same wisdom, the same spirit that inspired Abraham, Moses, and the prophets. However, because the term "spirit" has been defined by others in many subjective ways and has come to mean many different things to many people, this book will continue to refer to God's wisdom.

Another term for expressing good according to God's wisdom is love. But again it might cause undue confusion. Although there would be no attempt here to use that term subjectively, an objective usage is contrary to people's ordinary usage of love. It seems better for now to avoid the potential for confusion as much as possible. In this objective context, love would be actively pursuing the objective value good—that is, a pursuit of God's wisdom—and would not be defined by any subjective human emotion, desire, or motive.

It is sufficient to observe that, as the term love would be used here, it would be defined by the objective evidence of what God has done. As an example of God-defining love, see 1 John 4:19: "We love, because he [God] first loved us." God the Creator's love is evident in creation and its prospect for life. See also John 15:9–11 regarding the equivalence of love as taught by Jesus acting according to what God deems good in keeping His commandments.

The axiom that God is good therefore is the third proposed axiom. It describes in an elemental and useful way of an objective, substantive value inhering in the real context of life.

The axiom that God is good, together with the axiom that God is one, suggests that God alone establishes what is good and God alone is good. See, for example, Mark 10:18: "And Jesus said to him, 'Why do you call me good? No one is good but God alone.'" There is only one objective understanding of what is good and not many subjective ideas about it.

Although humans, along with the rest of creation, have been created good because we are part of and have a role in God's creation (Gen. 1:31), it does not follow that everything humans do is automatically good. There is no transitive property of good in that way. The fact that it is good that people, like any other part of creation, exist and that they, like every other creature, have a natural place and purpose in creation doesn't mean that people always choose to live within and according to that natural context instead of according to some human-created world and wisdom.

The fundamental dilemma of mankind generally is not that humans are somehow born inherently evil, as if anything that God made was not good, as idealistic theologians have maintained in their doctrine of original sin. The fact that people do evil is not because they are evil, but because they are misled or deceived into pursuing human desires and worlds. They do not live according to God's natural context in His wisdom and, having become a slave to their illusions and trying to do what they in their illusions perceive to be right, they have taught their illusions to their children, generation after generation.

This book is, like Jesus and Moses were, concerned with decisively breaking with that tradition of illusion in favor of the truth. The pursuit of understanding the natural and only true context for life is the first step to being able to live righteously within and according to God the Creator's natural order, whatever that order may objectively be discovered to be.

SUMMATION

Unless any other axiom can be demonstrated to add something objective to the effort, the three axioms discussed in this chapter seem sufficient for describing all we need to know to begin orienting life to its natural context.

These axioms should look familiar to Jews, Christians, and many others, but they aren't understood here in any idealistic or subjective way as many have previously understood them. As their derivation has demonstrated, these are neither assumed statements of subjective faith nor are they attempts to describe anything about God's "being." Most importantly, they aren't principles or ideals for creating an artificial world; they are working axioms for understanding the natural world and how to adapt to it. They have the functional and practical purpose of orienting life to its essential, natural context.

As derived, these axioms do not require further definition or enhancement by any subjective human description of God, good, or anything else. Subjective additions would only mislead, project illusions, and superimpose illusions over reality. As the axioms stand, objectively defined by the natural world, they offer a fundamental understanding of the natural world and how it works as the essential practical context for life, free from imagined and illusory contexts and orders.

This fundamental understanding expressed in axioms needs to be fleshed out, of course, by discovering the natural world and using the objective process to test understanding. That will naturally include scientific understanding to assist in ordering human life to its natural context.

A faith and way of life built on and oriented to this worldview is solidly founded. It is founded on what is real and true as best as we can know it. There is no subjectivity, artificiality, illusions, or doubts. This worldview stands independent of us, our imagination and subjectivity, our will, and our strengths and weaknesses.

This book makes no assertion that these axioms account for everything presented in the Bible. However, it does assert that these axioms describe the basic worldview of the Bible and, as such, that they are the fundamental bases of the core messages of both the Old and New Testaments. This will become more apparent throughout the remainder of this book, but for now it may be helpful to also observe, for example, that when Jesus was asked which commandment was the greatest, he said, "The first is 'Hear, O Israel: The Lord our God [understood as the Creator, the first axiom], the Lord is one [second axiom]; and you shall love the Lord your God with all your heart, and with all your soul, with all your mind and with all your strength [a statement of the third axiom in terms of love, a will to do good].' The second is this, 'You shall love your neighbor as yourself [again an objective will to do good].' There are no other commandments greater than these" (Mark 12:29–31).

The citations by Jesus are from Deuteronomy 6:4 and Leviticus 19:18, respectively.

See also Matthew 22:34–39 as a parallel to the passage from Mark. Note that Matthew's version, although more abbreviated, effectively restates the same axioms. It also asserts that the second commandment is "like the first." As will be demonstrated in the next chapter, the second derives from the first and is part of the expression of the first. Matthew then adds, "On these two commandments depend all the law and the prophets" (Matt. 22:40), and that also will be generally demonstrated.

The Gospel of Mark also reports that when the scribe, who had put the question to Jesus regarding the greatest commandment, wisely agreed with the answer, Jesus said to the scribe, "You are not far from the kingdom of God" (Mark 12:32–34). That understanding of a kingdom, where God the Creator's natural context for life rules practical decisions and God is effectively king, having exclusively established the order by which life in that context operates, is the next logical step and will be addressed in the next chapter.

CHAPTER 5

The Vision

THE TERM "VISION" as it relates to the natural world does not refer to some product of the human imagination. It derives from the foundations discussed Chapter 4 and is likewise a product of objective testing for its verification. It is the tested perception of how life is oriented to its natural context, where practical choices are governed by good as good is objectively understood, that is, by God's wisdom.

Pursuing the wisdom of God naturally implies the following:

» living harmoniously, not only with the underlying order that we could not change or affect anyway, but also with the consequences it has produced and would produce naturally on its own in the absence of destructive human efforts to try to impose a different, artificial world;

» healing the destructiveness perpetrated on the world by the pursuit of human wisdom and artificial worlds;

» imitating the natural order by enhancing life according to its order, helping to make life complete in its natural maturity and diversity;

» supporting others' efforts to live according to the natural worldview; and

» persuading others to live in and according to the natural world or, failing that, encouraging them to do such good as they will.

That list is not exclusive. God's wisdom also implies, for example, an attempt to understand the natural order in more detail, including an objective scientific understanding. The natural sciences are sister disciplines and supplement this effort. The supplementation is in a natural way, however, and not through any subjective definition or application of natural laws. For example, laws of natural selection and survival of the fittest are not to be assigned artificial definitions, such as what constitutes "the fittest." The laws need to be understood in nature's terms of whatever is most fit for any species' survival within the scheme of the natural order. Humans, like any other species, bring their intelligence and adaptability to the task. Such natural laws therefore also beg the adaptation that is intended to be discovered herein.

God's wisdom also implies a need for understanding to be drawn from direct human interaction with the natural order, which is referred to herein as natural law. Natural law includes, for example, obvious behaviors such as the need to kill for food within the broad purpose to promote life as nature promotes life. Such a survival choice is not the same, of course, as trying to re-create the world as we might prefer, and it is not an expression of any freedom or license to exploit creation simply because we can. It is an expression of the existence and maintenance of human life with the necessities that any species requires, and it suggests the intelligent promotion of a natural balance of all life. Other natural laws will be discussed in the next chapter.

Another example notably absent from that list is the imitation of natural disasters. There are at least two major reasons for that absence. The first is that, except in a few cases, humans are not yet wise enough to know when some forms of limited destruction generally promote life rather than destroy it or make it worse. In any event, the intricacies of predicting those consequences seem to involve more adequate scientific understanding than anything else, which is beyond the scope of this book.

The second major reason is that, if we were wise enough to make the correct decision, adequate safeguards are needed to assure that what is being done is in fact in the pursuit of God's wisdom. The repeated destructions perpetrated on the world throughout history in God's name under rallying calls such as "God is on our side," when God's wisdom never entered into much less guided the thought process, are too numerous to mention and too compelling to ignore. Safeguards would be a question of internal implementation, which is the subject of the next chapter.

Although good is objectively directed toward all of creation, the remainder of this book will nevertheless focus more narrowly on the specific implications among humans. The narrowed focus here should not be interpreted either as an abandonment of the pursuit of good toward the rest of the world or as any kind of artificial prioritization between doing good toward fellow humans and doing good toward the rest of the world.

The purpose of focusing on the implications for humans should, however, provide a more complete base of understanding how people can effectively work together and individually to adapt to the natural context of life, and accomplish good in and according to that context. It also should make it easier for some to begin to understand what may be involved in doing good according to God's wisdom.

BASICS

The choice to do good, as we are able, naturally involves humbling our individual subjective desires to God's wisdom, uncompromised by any form of human wisdom. The uncompromised humility might seem harsh to those accustomed to the extremes of idealistic systems, but such humility is neither alien to us nor anything unduly taxing of our ability. As a practical matter, people already practice a similar humility every day in whatever kind of political milieu they find themselves by submitting to any rule of law or form of government.

Even in a modern democracy founded on a theory of an individualized, arrogant, and fully independent noble savage, individual desires ultimately must be subordinated and humbled to the collective social desire expressed in the law of the land. Law-abiding citizens are humble citizens, even if they aren't so humble in other respects. Law-abiding humility is practical, whatever the social context.

If we can be humble to artificial, fictional contexts and the oppressive laws they prescribe, is it extreme to humble ourselves to the only real context for life that exists and to its ways and laws which produce and enhance life including our own?

When several people choose to act humbly according to

God's wisdom, there is not only a common goal of good among them but also a reciprocity of doing good toward each other. This common goal and reciprocity is the genesis of a vision of social interaction and community within life's natural context. It will generate a fundamental structure of social community. It will produce an understanding of a people who are, for all practical purposes, ruled by the order established by God, free from enslavement to human illusions and their attendant tyrannies. It is life as life was meant to be in its natural context. It is, in sum, a vision of the kingdom of God, and it was the vision of Moses and Jesus.

Internally among those who choose this natural context, a common and reciprocal pursuit of good naturally requires at least two or three people to function. Note Matthew 18:20: "For where two or three are gathered in my name, there I am in the midst of them." Gathering in the name of Jesus is, as a practical matter, gathering in the spirit of what Jesus taught, the wisdom and spirit of God. The more people who engage in reciprocating good, of course, the more diverse, capable, and complete the reciprocity can be in meeting more kinds of needs.

The term "needs" as used in this context is not intended to refer only to the bare necessities for sustaining life. It is used in a broader sense to refer to anything people may objectively need to become the mature, full, complete, unique individuals they can be. It includes people's potential for wisdom and skills useful to function practically in and to the benefit of this natural context of life.

Anyone's efforts to do good, to meet the needs of others, is exemplified in one respect by the model of the voluntary, humble servant undertaking to serve the needs of others according to his or her abilities. That sense of humility and servitude is not, however, in the sense of subjecting himself or herself to the superiority, whims, indignities, abuses, and demands of another person. It is not a matter of relative human status or following orders based on such a status. It is not a matter of embarrassment, self-doubt, or groveling. This is not servitude as human wisdom typically defines it. Here, the servant essentially is in control of the type, extent, or manner of service.

The servitude is most basically to God in the form of the effort to do good in the natural context that God has created, which includes fellow humans. It serves the natural context that serves all life in producing and maintaining life, including ourselves. The humility is not to other people as such, except in the sense of holding their needs as important as, or in some cases more important than, our own needs and positioning ourselves to perceive others' needs as well as we can. The servitude is, in its most mature practice and understanding, based in solid objective understanding of needs and expressed in a masterful ability to enhance and contribute to the life and welfare of others and all creation.

Jesus is a prime example of this and taught his followers accordingly. See Mark 10:42–45: "And Jesus called them to him and said to them, 'You know that those who are supposed to rule over the Gentiles lord it over them. But it shall not be so among you; but whoever would be great among you must be your servant, and whoever would be first among you must be slave of all.'" John 13:1–15 details Jesus' example of serving: washing his disciples' feet. Philippians 2:4–5 says, "Let each of you look not only to his own interests but also to the interests of others. Have this mind among yourselves, which is yours in Christ Jesus."

Because of the reciprocity of good, it is advantageous for everyone in this community that there be as many diverse talents as possible, used with maturity and efficiency, for meeting their individual and collective needs. The goal of meeting needs thereby encourages everyone to enhance others' individual welfare and growth in all forms of education and maturity and, with it, the maturity of the community as well to the benefit of all. As will be discussed later, the natural interdependence and goodwill of this community as a whole encourages cooperative efforts to meet additional social needs that individuals alone could not meet.

Within the community of those who share this vision, all who are served are servants, reciprocally. All reciprocal servants are of equal human dignity, all serving and being served by each other according to their respective abilities and needs. The general equality of status that results within the community is more easily seen in New Testament texts that contrast life under God's wisdom with life under human wisdom, although in some texts better than in others. See, for example, 1 Corinthians 7:17–24 where Paul talks about those who are slaves in their socioeconomic relations outside the church being free and equal within the church.

That general equality among church members is, unfortunately, not as clear in the New Testament in respect to women. Understanding why the confusion exists requires a bit of jumping ahead into implementation issues, yet it can be introduced here in terms of the vision insofar as God's wisdom makes no distinctions, except those that exist objectively in nature. All other distinctions are artificial stereotypes, and all other divisions are artificial divisions between people. Note Galatians 3:28: "There is neither Jew nor Greek; there is neither slave nor free; there is neither male nor female; for you are all one in Christ Jesus."

Conflicting practice nevertheless developed as a matter of

implementation because of the need of the church to convert and teach those with entrenched prejudices introduced by human wisdom. Persuading them involves seeing to their needs without putting stumbling blocks in their way. For the sake of new converts as well, who were yet immature in God's wisdom and would find offense at gender equality, which might unduly affect their continued membership and growth in God's wisdom, a temporary indulgence served their needs. No one new to the community can be expected to be mature in God's wisdom immediately, so this and many other types of temporary indulgence serve that purpose—but only that purpose. It is neither an adoption of human wisdom nor an excuse to remain immature in God's wisdom.

Historically, it can be said with confidence that women enjoyed considerable opportunity and status within the original following of Jesus that was not enjoyed elsewhere. For example, Jesus not only included women among his closest followers, but he also taught women at a time when education, beyond a minimal level, was for men only (see Luke 10:38–42). Education is, of course, an essential step in breaking down and eliminating barriers between the artificial classes of privileged and underprivileged as well as in revealing all forms of human wisdom for the fictions they are. Note also 1 Corinthians 7:3–5 in respect to an equal, reciprocal humility between husband and wife within the Christian marriage.

As with every other effort to do good, defined objectively, the perception and fulfillment of another's needs is best determined objectively instead of subjectively. Objectivity requires testing against nature's standards, which may involve a lengthy learning process. In the meantime, a subjective effort is better than none at all, especially when guided by less formal but relatively effective guidelines for reciprocal behavior, such as the Golden Rule: "So whatever you wish that men would do to you, do so to them; for this is the law and the prophets" (Matt. 7:12). This works easily with common needs, but it can also work in respect to meeting more specialized needs.

A second model for objectively meeting others' needs is that of a wise and nurturing parent exercising sound judgment for the welfare of his or her child to help that child to mature. The wise parent does not give the child whatever the child immaturely or subjectively perceives to be its own needs, however much the parent loves the child and empathizes with the child's desires. Instead, the wise and loving parent tries to learn about the child's genuine needs and neither to ignore those needs nor spoil the child by substituting ineffective gestures. The wise parent will humble himself or herself not to the child's immature judgment or pretenses but to his or her real needs and will try to meet them with whatever resources are available. The parent also may indulge the child and give into the child's desires occasionally, of course, particularly when it does encourage the child's maturity, but that is in addition to and never a substitute for what can be done to meet the child's genuine needs.

If adults can provide small children's needs, immaturely expressed to them and without any expectancy of reciprocal benefit, they can certainly do the same or better for more adults who usually will understand and express their own needs and, in the broad context of the community, reciprocally care for them.

The objective perception of needs and recognition of ways to meet needs are, like every other subject of objective knowledge, learned talents. Some people will be more talented at it than others, and some can be more specialized than others, but all can improve as part of the community's educational goals. Education as a part of implementation will be discussed in the next chapter.

The ways in which people can do good have as much variety and efficacy as their own natural talents and maturity allow. Talents and abilities naturally vary considerably, which is good because needs vary considerably as well.

Efforts to do good would ordinarily, but need not always, be in the form of directly helping others. Some efforts also may be indirect and perhaps less tangible, depending on where individual talents lie. Those indirect benefits include, for example, the advancement of knowledge and scholarship as well as objective testing. These may prove as important to the community's ultimate goals in pursuit of God's wisdom as any other, more direct effort. Indirect efforts are not, of course, intended to be to the exclusion of more direct participation in the community's day-to-day life.

Anyone's contributions in doing good are not properly appreciated or measured according to any artificial standard of comparison. All contributions should be appreciated for the natural standard of whatever individuals have the ability to offer. Note, for example, Mark 12:41–44, where a poor widow, who contributed two small copper coins, which was much less than others, was praised as one who gave the most because, by a natural measure, she gave everything she had. That doesn't apply only to money or assets; it applies to every resource at one's disposal, including natural abilities.

The reciprocity of good also is best understood as voluntary, as essentially a gift. Although there is a natural incentive and expectation of a general reciprocal benefit in having our own needs met as a member of such a community, doing good to another is not conditional. There is no direct or implied bargaining or buying and selling of the reciprocity of good.

Whatever good one may receive as part of the diverse community may come from entirely different people from those one serves. Every member, though sharing a common goodwill, has unique needs and unique abilities to meet needs. There is no expectancy of equal give and take between individuals, no bilateral contract and no *quid pro quo*. The vision of a maturely developed community is not one of equal reciprocity between individuals but a reciprocity of meeting needs that is effected throughout the entirety of a diverse, organic community. Any individual effort to do good is naturally dependent on being served according to our needs. Everyone needs to be nurtured, sustained, and refreshed. We cannot serve others indefinitely without it, just as we need food for sustained physical effort. The willing receipt of good from others is essential to individual growth and maturity.

Being receptive of the good others offer is an expression of participation in doing good and another aspect of the same humility to the community's objective goals. Receiving from others requires a measure of acceptance of, reliance on, and faith in others' and the community's objective judgment as a whole that what is offered is good for one's needs. See Matthew 6:25–33.

> Therefore I tell you, do not be anxious about your life, what you eat or what you shall drink, nor about your body, what you shall put on. Is not life more than food, and the body more than clothing? Look at the birds of the air; they neither sow nor reap nor gather into barns, and yet your heavenly Father feeds them. Are you not of more value than they? And which of you by being anxious can add one cubit to his

span of life? And why are you anxious about clothing? Consider the lilies of the field, how they grow; they neither toil nor spin; yet I tell you, even Solomon in all his glory was not arrayed like one of these ... But seek first his kingdom and his righteousness, and all these things shall be yours as well.

The model for receiving good is not that of the arrogant, prideful, and dictatorial lord and master of the servant, as in human wisdom. To the contrary, it is that of the meek, accepting little child—the reciprocal of the loving parent. A child receives good from others, relying on others to give him or her what is objectively needed without any ability to reciprocate. (It is a mistake to surmise that the biblical example of a child is a reference to some notion that childish immaturity or ignorance is somehow something Christians should desire. Simple-mindedness is a vulnerability to being led astray [Rom. 16:18]. Maturity is to be desired [Eph. 4:12–14; Heb. 5:12–14].)

Meekness in this context is not understood, as human wisdom ordinarily defines it as weak, unassertive, and ineffectual. It refers instead to the community's humility toward God and the natural context of life, not arrogating our own desires and seeking self-power to try to manipulate people and situations to accomplish selfish desires and create and live in an artificial world of our own preference. It is a humility toward what is real, doing good, and accepting others' efforts to do good. While that meekness abhors any strength to grasp for ourselves at the expense of others, it supports the maturity of character, will, and ability to serve others intelligently and energetically.

The reference to the meek inheriting the earth (Matt. 5:5)

seems to embrace two ideas in this regard: that those who humbly accept the world as God made it try to live within it instead of trying to create a different world, and that everyone around the world will eventually give up human fictions and illusions in favor of the context of the natural world.

Reliance upon others to fulfill one's needs is not intended to require deprivation if others might not meet every need in a timely way. Self-help is not forbidden. Because each person is part of creation, which is to be served by doing good, it is proper to do good for ourselves as well. In some circumstances, self-help or self-support is necessary. An example is a missionary who may be living substantially outside of and away from the community where there is little or no reciprocity of meeting needs. It is important, however, that self-help remain in proper context and perspective, and not be artificially arrogated to a value in and of itself.

It is tempting to take the idea of self-help out of context, ascribe an artificial value to the relative ability to care for ourselves, and construct an artificial context for life based in part on that idea. Despite a person's ability to care for himself or herself independently in many ways, reliance on self-help tends to invoke subjective decisions instead of objective ones. It tends to change the focus from doing good as defined objectively into some other artificially and subjectively defined idea that good is self-serving. For these, and perhaps other reasons, resorting to self-help needs to be viewed more as an exception than the rule.

Individuals' maturity in this social order likewise is not defined by the ability to be independent or self-sufficient; it is defined by natural standards and involves two aspects. First, maturity involves becoming the complete person we were created to be and acting accordingly. It is a realistic goal that every individual can achieve if given help and opportunity, and that help and opportunity is encouraged here insofar as any person's maturity is in everyone else's interests as well as the interests of the world generally. This maturity is no ideal, of course. It is realistic. It demands no more or less of a person than what is within him or her to do, according to his or her abilities.

A second kind of maturity also varies from person to person according to natural abilities and will be enhanced by study and experience. It involves objectively discerning the natural context of life according to this discipline, understanding what is good and what is not, and being willing to pursue good and only good. It is a maturity in God's wisdom, and the greatest extent of maturity in this respect is especially desirable for teachers and others in a position of leadership.

God's wisdom is not a wisdom anyone necessarily has by virtue of the first kind of maturity. For example, adults who are new to this way of life and whose individual skills and abilities already may have been well developed need to be nurtured, educated, and oriented to a way of life that is as new to them as it would be to a newborn child. See, for example, John 3:1–12, where Jesus expected the Jewish leader, Nicodemus, to understand the concept of being born again. The reference was neither to a physical rebirth nor to a return to a newborn child's mental ignorance and general incompetence. The concept referred to the Jewish practice, which Jesus expected Nicodemus to know, of educating and orienting new converts to Judaism to an entirely new and different socioreligious perspective, leaving their divergent ways behind and adopting a new and different way of thinking and behaving. It was entering into a new context of life, a new way of life, a new need to mature in a different wisdom. See also 1 Corinthians

3:1–2: "But I, brethren, could not address you as spiritual men, but as men of the flesh, as babes in Christ. I fed you with milk, not solid food; for you were not ready for it; and even yet you are not ready."

The concept of individual perfection within this context similarly does not refer to some abstract, artificial, and unrealistic ideal or standard such as freedom from error for all time or a particular length of time. Instead, perfection is understood in the practical and natural sense of completeness according to one's natural abilities and capacity for understanding and living according to God's wisdom. An individual is perfect if he or she is the mature (or maturing) creature he or she has the ability to be within God's natural context of life.

MEMBERSHIP

Membership in this community is identified by the voluntary commitment to living in the natural context of life that embraces the entire universe. It is not confined to any territory.

Membership also is not determined by any recitation of abstract beliefs or mere claim of allegiance. Note Matthew 7:15–20. The evidence and proof is in actions, not words.

All who similarly do good are in fact our welcome neighbors, whether or not artificial differences and distinctions still exist. See, for example, Jesus' story of the Good Samaritan in response to the question of "Who is my neighbor?" (Luke 10:29–37).

Doing good with any degree of consistency requires a purposeful design and commitment to do so. The example of a Samaritan was no accident. Samaritans weren't just any kind of ignorant or despised foreigner. They also believed in God the Creator, considered Moses to be the great prophet, and accepted the Torah. It was not surprising that a Samaritan would do good despite the political and other superficial differences and accusations of corrupted beliefs that alienated Samaritans from Jews.

Jesus' example includes Samaritans, or anyone else, based on the like commitment to do good beyond the isolated or occasional instance. Labels and stereotypes don't control membership. It shouldn't matter what a person calls himself or herself religiously or otherwise. Substance controls over form.

Similarly, those who claim membership by way of belief but who do not exhibit that commitment by their actions and attempt to mature are not true members for the very reason that their own actions place them outside of the community. See Matthew 7:21: "Not every one who *says* to me, 'Lord, Lord,' shall enter the kingdom of heaven, but he who *does* the will of my Father who is in heaven" (emphasis added). See also Matthew 21:28–31.

An extreme example is in Matthew 12:46–50: "While he was still speaking to the people, behold, his mother and his brothers stood outside, asking to speak to him. But he replied to the man who told him, 'Who is my mother, and who are my brothers?' And stretching out his hand toward his disciples, he said, 'Here are my mother and my brothers! For whoever *does* the will of my Father in heaven is my brother, and sister, and mother'" (emphasis added).

The ritualized Christian expression of this rebirth and new beginning in a new way of life—the symbolic drowning or killing of the old life and emerging into a new life—is baptism. The real, practical substance is not in the ritual, as if this were a resort to a magical worldview. The substance of it is in a real, tangible change of our way of life, ritually marked by a new beginning and new direction in a new practical context.

It has to be a full change of our way of making practical decisions. The acceptance of the natural context of life does not allow for inclusion as well of artificial contexts with their countervailing values and goals. They can't fit with each other without effectively creating in the merging process an entirely new fictional context for life. The result would effectively be a rejection of the natural context of life in favor of yet another fiction. To use a metaphor attributed to Jesus, putting new wine into old wineskins doesn't work.

Trying to put a way of life based on a natural context into an artificial context or vice versa is impossible. The choice is either for or against the natural context of life. Stated in the practical terminology of the axioms, God is one. There are no other gods to follow.

A person can follow one context for life faithfully but not more. To paraphrase another one of Jesus' metaphors, a person might serve one master and be diplomatically friendly and respectful toward another, just as exist today between two different countries based in different artificial worlds, but one cannot serve two masters faithfully at the same time. See Matthew 6:24: "No one can serve two masters; for either he will hate the one and love the other, or he will be devoted to the one and despise the other. You cannot serve God and mammon."

Mammon usually is interpreted as wealth but, in a broader sense, it represents any artificial value or human desire that might serve as our master in lieu of God the Creator. The point is again that God is one, the only master.

Because the change to a natural context of life is so different for the new member, it requires an opportunity to change with nothing done under the prior way of life held against him or her. Practicality requires forgiving the new member for everything that preceded, everything done according to the old context and way of thinking, because nothing done in that context could have been expected to be good or wise according to the new context. With forgiveness, there is the genuine opportunity for a new start and meaningful support for a new and better life free from the past.

Leaving the old, familiar way for something new and unfamiliar is difficult enough. The initial function of forgiveness is to let an individual enter this new social order uninhibited. Nothing prevents a better future quite like stubbornly forcing someone to live according to or be held accountable for an undesirable past. People can't change the past for the better; people can change only their present and future for the better.

There naturally may be some residual wariness because of a new member's special past in order to avoid vulnerability to an immature, untested, and perhaps ambiguously committed new member. Indeed, such watchfulness is essential to encouraging growth in God's wisdom.

To that end, however, there is the opportunity for a new start with all the help the community can offer. Recall the wariness of the early church in respect to Paul who, before converting, had persecuted Christians (Acts 9:1–26). Without forgiveness, he never would have had the opportunity to change. We also benefit immensely because of it.

To secure a fresh start, this forgiveness must be reciprocal. A new member's entry into the community is a commitment as well to forgive every wrong or perceived wrong committed by any other member of the community. The reasons the new member should forgive, however, may have more to do with two other functions of forgiveness.

A second function of forgiveness within the community is similar to the first: to allow the process of maturity within the community to occur without letting the failures of immaturity and old habits cause others to stop maturing. There is no practical expectancy that people will fully change and mature overnight, even if they honestly undertake a dedicated pursuit of God's wisdom. They must learn new ways of thinking and acting, which takes time. Even adults new to this way, like a child, must able to grow and make mistakes before full maturity can be expected. Mistakes continue throughout life, of course, so we always need forgiveness.

A third function of forgiveness is to begin the process of healing damaged relationships caused by past mistakes and allow the parties to move forward to a better future. In the absence of forgiveness, past errors and injuries continue to loom and prevent the parties from moving forward with reciprocal goodwill toward one another. Therefore, as difficult as it may be emotionally for those injured by past mistakes, forgiveness must begin the process of recouping a genuine reciprocal goodwill.

Forgiveness alone does not complete the healing process. Forgiveness provides only an opportunity—but a necessary opportunity. We cannot heal while reserving any opportunity to do further injury toward our neighbor or refusing to let a wound heal. For example, Matthew 18:21–22 states, "Then Peter came up and said to him, 'Lord, how often shall my brother sin against me, and I forgive him? As many as seven times?' Jesus said to him, 'I do not say to you seven times, but seventy times seven.'"

Mending and healing wounds requires additional effort that is consistent with and part of the community's essential nature to do good toward one another to fill needs. Forgiveness following injury therefore allows the community to return to that dynamic function without distraction. More specific dynamics of the healing processes in the case of injury or wrongdoing will be addressed in the next chapter on implementation under the topics of discipline and dispute resolution. Those procedures will likewise take on different perspectives and functions consistent with this context, distinct from the way artificial contexts and human wisdom would pursue them.

Forgiveness is the practical thing to do in this context. In contrast to perpetuating and spreading resentment by exacting retribution, it bears repeating that forgiveness allows relationships within the community to look forward and improve on the present situation. In whatever condition the community finds itself, for whatever reasons, the goal is to proceed from there to enhance life as much as possible.

Therefore, forgiveness is not an idealistic or abstract theological concept, a conscience cleanser, an excuse or a superficial ritual that allows someone to return to or repeat the same errant life as before. It doesn't tacitly approve acts of ill will or maintain an unfair status quo. It is a practical and essential first step in the process of returning to doing good, as individuals and a community, improving the situation whatever it may be, overcoming the effects of errors as best can be done under the circumstances.

Refusal to forgive is therefore contrary to the community's nature and is a potential reason for exclusion from the community, at least until such time as the person is ready to forgive and return to the pursuit of God's wisdom. This and other reasons to exclude someone from the community are addressed in more detail in the next chapter.

PERSONAL RELATIONS

The effort to do good and help each other to mature is beneficial for all sorts of personal relationships that would not otherwise exist or would exist only at a guarded distance. When others have our interests at heart rather than just their own, there is no need to build barriers to protect ourselves from potential exploitation and injury or tear down anyone else. In the dynamics of this community, weaknesses are reasons to build and strengthen instead of exploit. We are free to accept others with confidence that our own vulnerability will not be exploited but will be part of the reason to interact positively.

Prospective friends likewise no longer must fit into a narrow, familiar mold of behavior and attitudes that, by experience in a hostile, competitive, and back-stabbing artificial world, have proved to be relatively familiar and safe. In their natural context, people can become open to others who genuinely have the others' good interests at heart.

Without the need to be defensive, relationships between people can be more realistic, honest, open, and meaningful. They can be based on who people truly are, not on how they want others to think of them according to some unrealistic ideal or other artificial social standard. The only standard people must meet is working commonly and reciprocally toward becoming the mature people they were born to be. Emotional ties are free to exist positively with fewer reservations and less of a likelihood of false expectations and disappointment.

There also is no place for stereotypes or other artificial categorizations to be projected on others, pigeon-holing them because of artificially established expectations. All artificial standards of judgment are rejected in favor of accepting people for who they are and who they can be when living in and according to the natural context of life. When someone falls short of achieving what they can, it is a reason for assistance, not distance.

This lack of artificial expectancies, along with healing and forgiveness, allows people to change, grow, and mature. There is no need to judge from the first impression. There is no need to judge at any time except to meet needs and do good. If there is any shortcoming, it is a reason for helping and including instead of exploiting or excluding.

People are free to be what their nature, heart, and soul leads them to be. They are free to pursue their real talents and abilities, and they have the help of others in fulfilling every need to become all they can be. They can do this free from the oppression, repression, barriers, and pitfalls of artificial social orders.

COOPERATION

When people have each other's interests at heart and forgive others for wrongdoing, they naturally cooperate with each other to coordinate their efforts to achieve greater good. The cooperative effort to do good promotes the efficient and circumspect use of resources, both human and natural, to meet needs. No artificial incentive is needed to promote cooperation, and no artificial incentive of self-interest operates to pervert or undermine the cooperative effort. All types of cooperation and coordination necessary or useful for the community to serve are naturally encouraged.

The New Testament church, for example, moved rather quickly to organizing its talents to meet basic needs for food, clothing, preaching, and teaching. See Acts 6:1–5 regarding feeding the poor, assignment of the job to mature people, while other mature members could devote themselves to prayer and ministry according to their gifted abilities. See also Ephesians 4:11–16.

And his gifts were that some should be apostles, some prophets, some evangelists, some pastors and teachers, to equip the saints for the work of ministry, for building up the body of Christ until we all attain to the unity of faith and of the knowledge of the Son of God, to mature manhood, to the measure of the stature of the fullness of Christ; so that we may no longer be children, tossed to and fro and carried with every wind of doctrine, by the cunning of men, by their craftiness in deceitful wiles. Rather, speaking the truth in love, we are to grow up in every way into him who is the head, into Christ, from whom the whole body, joined and knit together by every joint with which it is supplied, when each part is working properly, makes bodily growth and upbuilds itself in love.

That mutual goodwill also improves organizational and group dynamics. When people have each other's interests at heart, there can be a division and assignment of responsibilities according to genuine ability and maturity instead of according to artificial, efficacy-defeating yardsticks, such as popularity, image, nepotism, bias, age, longevity, ambition, and self-promotion. Those who are mature and tested (see Chapter 8) and have been given responsibility within an organization or group can likewise be trusted to exercise that responsibility humbly for the good of others and creation as a whole instead of arrogantly for their own selfish interests. Organization, development, and the use of human and other resources is therefore more natural, expert, and efficient.

When people have others' interests at heart, ideas and contributions may be truly valued on their own objective merit. Everything beneficial can be honestly tested and encouraged accordingly, free of ulterior motives generated by a dynamic of self-interest, self-promotion, and the pursuit of other subjective values.

Economics

The community's most basic economic dynamic already has been addressed in terms of reciprocity and cooperation, but that dynamic has some important implications. For example, this economic system works with humans as part of the natural world, part of the environment God created, instead of separate from and arrogantly above it. The system is inherently ecological as opposed to offering artificial incentives for exploiting nature mercilessly for vain, arrogant desires and then becoming ecologically minded only when utter desperation for survival, caused by the mistreatment of the environment by that artificial system, demands it.

The community's economics is inherently supportive of people as well. It doesn't exploit or manipulate people as impersonal raw resources to be exhausted and expended.

Another basic economic difference from artificial systems can be illustrated in differing concepts of economic waste. We can get an idea of what an economy fundamentally values by what it considers waste. Economic waste in an artificial context is defined as the failure to convert the use of some type of property to some human purpose that the artificial context values. In a natural economy, waste is understood as not using an asset wisely according to God's wisdom. Use for a human purpose, value, or wisdom, except as may coincidentally be consistent with God's wisdom, constitutes waste in this natural context.

Another example is that, in the ordinary capitalistic system, a seller's profit interest tends to be made most important and legally protected over competing interests because, if a product or service is not profitable, it isn't offered regardless of how much is it needed. Because profit determines availability, products and services aren't necessarily what is needed in a particular case or what someone in need can afford. In the natural economy, need and anticipated need determines the products or services to be offered to anyone. Products and services are limited only by the human and natural resources that may be available to supply them.

In a natural context, economics directly addresses doing good, which includes meeting real needs, human and environmental, and moving and using resources accordingly. It doesn't move resources according to artificial standards of profit taking, which more often than not moves resources toward artificial wealth and less often toward any real need. The allocation of resources isn't skewed toward the artificially rich, who may purchase what they desire and do not need while the artificially poor may never get what they need.

Natural economic efficiency lies in the effective use of resources for doing good. It uses resources to build up the natural world instead of exploiting it to build up a fiction.

Note that competition becomes a problem in an artificial context primarily insofar as it may pit one person against another to earn a profit from which to survive at the other's expense. This tends to create contempt or ill will toward one another and the natural world. Whether a healthy competition might serve some other function within a community of goodwill, for example, to sharpen skills or compare qualifications meritoriously, remains for experience and testing to answer.

The concept of property also changes somewhat. The real

issue is again in how property is used, just as in respect to how our own talents and abilities are used. Assets also should be used according to God's wisdom. Property ownership would be more analogous to what capitalistic economies would call a trusteeship rather than strict ownership. In effect, God is the owner and the property is used for His purposes, where the trustee decides for what purpose in any individual situation.

This different thinking about property is not a characterization of individual property as community or government property. There may be common property held by the government, just as there is in any modern capitalistic society, but it is hardly a requirement. To suggest that all property is automatically common property is counterproductive to the community's purposes.

Central ownership may, of course, offer some useful economic efficiencies, but it is not this community's character that a government either thinks or acts for everyone and renders its citizens its employees or subjects. The government is a form of implementation, as will be addressed more specifically in the next chapter. It exists to serve the people. It can suggest but not dictate the use of people's property, talents, or abilities.

Whether or not money, as an artificial species of property trading for artificially evaluated goods and services, might have any independent use within a system of common and reciprocal good seems doubtful in respect to a fully mature community, but that can remain an open question for now. Mainly, its current use would seem to be for any necessary or useful trade and commerce with outsiders who rely on it and for an interim use until the community is able to work internally without it. Dealing with external economic systems is an issue of external implementation.

Closing Observations

Although happiness was not an axiomatic value descriptive of the world and how it works, greater happiness is a natural result of this way of life. People whose needs are being met without having to struggle for them are happier. People who aren't continually victimized by others are happier. People who can be themselves and develop to their potential are happier. People who are useful to others and feel needed are happier. People in open, honest, natural, cooperative, and mutually beneficial relationships with others and nature are happier.

Observe that the reason we live this way isn't to feel good, although that may happen. The reason isn't to reap some reward in the afterlife, although that might also happen. The reason is that this is the realistic, wise way to adapt to the only real world there is, whatever collateral personal reward we may or may not gain.

More implications of this vision could be discussed, along with a wider variety of individual needs, but what has been discussed seems sufficient to present the general gist of the vision. The discussion has already anticipated several implementation issues, and internal implementation is the subject of the next chapter.

CHAPTER 6

Internal Implementation

P EOPLE WON'T AUTOMATICALLY understand and react appropriately to life's natural context. We aren't preprogrammed, instinctive creatures. We are thinking creatures, and we seldom have the time or self-discipline in our thinking even when we try to understand and react as best as we can to our practical context. We have limited past experience on which to draw conclusions. We are bombarded by many distractions and face many limitations that frustrate our best efforts.

Most of us know that it helps to develop good personal habits and guidelines for our own individual benefit, and an individual effort in accord with the worldview must certainly be encouraged. However, a collective effort is the focus of this chapter.

Internal implementation involves those strategies by which

a community of those adhering to the vision collectively organizes itself to accomplish its purposes and deal effectively with anything that may be anticipated to subvert or distract from its purposes. Internal implementation is an integral part of social life.

As necessary as implementation will be to a practical realization of life in accordance with the worldview and vision, there remains a critical distinction to be maintained. Implementation is not the community's goal; it is a means to promote that goal. The primary focus must remain on the worldview and vision to assure that any form of implementation, however poorly or brilliantly it may be designed or applied, supports its guiding purpose.

In choosing strategies, structures, and institutions that are helpful, the method of the discipline relies on experience and testing against nature's standards to select better means over time. Nevertheless, we don't have to start at this point without any ideas of what will likely work.

There are two major sources from which to get a head start. One source, which will provide a general outline of issues for this chapter, is to address strategies common to all forms of social organization in coping with analogous needs. It also should help to compare some similarities and contrast some differences in how one context or another affects the character and use of those means. The other major source is background biblical experience of what appears to have proven effective.

GOVERNMENT

In artificial contexts, government typically is the primary institutional means of addressing implementation. It creates and imposes the law, order, and hierarchy of society against internal dissension and serves as the people's agent regarding foreign relations. Discussion of government usually is considered a favorite topic, full of the lure of fame, power, and glory, and typically is the first issue people want to address.

Form needs to serve substantive function, so we need to address the function of government in a natural context first. Like other organizations in this natural community, government is an outgrowth of cooperating and coordinating efforts to do good efficiently. Government differs from other organizations only insofar as government action also constitutes the formal, official action of the entire community when, but only when, that kind of full cooperative effort is needed.

The functions of this government are more limited in purpose than governments pursuing fictional contexts. For example, because nature already has evidenced the order to be followed, and it can be said that God is functionally the king of the community in respect to having established the order, it is not a purpose of internal implementation either to add to or subtract from that natural context or its underlying substantive order. To do so would create an artificial context for life. Pursuit of the natural context leaves no other context to be created or imposed. There is therefore no need for a legislative type of function with which to create and establish a new or different law and order of the community. This also is an expression of the concept that God is one. See Deuteronomy 12:32: "Everything that I command you shall be careful to do; you shall not add to it or take from it." See also Matthew 5:19.

The function of achieving a better objective understanding of the natural world and how it works and, with that, articulating the best current expression of the community's law and order is fundamentally an academic function instead of a governmental one. It is for the continuing intellectual study of diverse individuals addressed to the objective discipline. It is to be discovered by the objective process, not to be created or preemptively decided and fixed subjectively by any singular human institution, as in artificial contexts. It is for the highest intelligence of mankind to discover, test understanding, and continue to refine the law's articulation as experience and understanding grows. That academic purpose naturally involves, but is not strictly limited to, the educational institution.

In respect to the personnel who will make governmental decisions on the community's behalf, whatever the decisions may be, they are best chosen according to the wisdom guiding the community. When people have each other's interests at heart, people want those who are most mature and dedicated to serving others to make the most important decisions. Those most capable to make decisions and exercise government functions must be those who have been tested (see Chapter 8) and demonstrated substantial maturity in God's wisdom. The goal is to make the best decisions according to God's wisdom, and that is application of an objective standard.

The process of choosing governmental personnel, and removing them if necessary to assure accountability to God's wisdom, also must lie in the hands of those who have achieved some maturity in God's wisdom. If personnel are to chosen by election, the electors also need some level of maturity in this area. No artificial criteria for election, such as popularity or kinship, should confuse that effort.

In respect to the decision-making process, experience has demonstrated that joint decision making is preferred over individual decision making. Joint decision making draws on broader knowledge, experience, and perspectives. It helps to assure that a careful and circumspect decision is made using the best evidence for the best objective reasons. Joint decision making also helps to avoid the potential for corruption and assure that those in authority act according to God's wisdom instead of self-interest, emotional prejudice, or another form of subjective corruption.

Joint decision making in this context will be more efficient than joint decision making in, for example, a democratic context. The reason is that, where the focus and rationale of decision making is on adhering to God's wisdom, it is objective in nature and there is no division of purpose. It is not, as in a democracy, a negotiation of wide-ranging personal subjective opinions and self-interests that each individual promotes and tries to negotiate to skew the results more favorably to his or her own interests.

Additionally, joint decision making in God's wisdom focuses more clearly and accurately on the real issues with a common goal. People can more readily agree when they focus on the same objective perspective and goal instead of on personal diverse and divisive subjective interests. Where a course of action is unclear because of a lack of experience, there should be general agreement to test, reject what doesn't work, and move on from there. See 1 Corinthians 1:10 and 2:16 as well as Philippians 1:27 and, as an expression of human humility and obedience to this one mind in God's wisdom, Philippians 2:1–8.

The procedures adopted for collective decision making need to encourage the wisest and most circumspect analysis to persuade and therefore prevail. A willingness to question everything intellectually is helpful to a full and circumspect consideration, although a desire merely to be divisive is not. Any debate in the course of decision making serves as a kind of preliminary test of the merits, but it is not a final test. Decisions ultimately need to be tested in context and experience against nature's standards, just as with everything else.

One useful model for discussing a proposal's merits is to allow the wisest and most experienced to speak last and the less mature and experienced to speak first. This allows for the least mature to gain valuable experience in hands-on analysis while also demonstrating a relative level of analytical skills to the rest. It allows the more mature to benefit from the widest range of considerations to which to add their own analysis, if any, and present their opportunity to persuade. The lesser mature then learn from the more mature as well as from their own efforts. The process avoids simply adopting the first articulated conclusion as correct because of its source, if the wiser were to speak first.

ECONOMICS

The community's basic internal economics were addressed in the previous chapter, but there are any number of implementation issues to address. A discussion of a few of the more obvious issues will be sufficient here.

This community is, of course, in everyone's self-interest, even if self-interest isn't the rule of individual economic behavior. Again, the question isn't what anyone might do for any reason if left to their own ignorant devices. This is a community effort to adapt to the natural world, and there is much more to be gained as part of the whole than as a separate, adverse individual.

The most obvious internal economic strategy is to create organizations and amass information to promote the economic coordination of skills and resources so that they are directed efficiently toward needs. This coordination does not have to be limited to a governmental organization. Although governmental organization might serve the community's more general, ordinary needs, more diverse needs call for more specialized maturity in respect to individual talents. A simple example is that medical needs would be met better by those with medical knowledge and talents, while the logistics of distributing medical services efficiently might be better met by those having the talents for practical logistics and coordination.

The most difficult internal economic problem to address may be the person who selfishly receives without contributing reciprocally according to his or her ability. The freeloader or idle person was a major concern among the first Christians. There are many references that people and local church organizations were expected to bear fruits. Fruits are the expected result of maturity in God's wisdom. It is a reflection of God's work in all creation, as the whole world bears fruit in its season (Col. 1:6). A failure to produce fruit evidences a lack of health and maturity (Luke 8:14–15). Note that there are, conversely, fruits of human wisdom as well: "Beware of false prophets, who come to you in sheep's clothing but inwardly are ravenous wolves. You will know them by their fruits" (Matt. 7:15–16).

Failure to contribute to the community negatively affects its efficiency, but a lack of participation in the community's basic dynamics presents the more serious problem of rejecting the community's basic vision. Such conduct may be so serious as to indicate that the individual desires to live outside this community. Failure to mature and bear fruit indicates either corruption or a lack of commitment, demonstrating that the person may lack the desire to be a part of the community. Such a lack of desire is grounds for formally recognizing the individual as effectively outside of the community. See, for example, John 15:1–6. There are also natural disciplinary measures short of cutting the person off from the community that will be discussed later in this chapter under the topic of discipline.

The immature obviously are not expected to contribute as much. Their abilities have not fully developed, and their efforts need to be spent on maturing. The mature accordingly need to accommodate the immature to encourage their maturation. Nevertheless, every person is capable of some effort according to his or her existing abilities, and that includes maturing seasonably according to one's talents and abilities.

For those who cannot or will not mature, for example, by continuing to be greedy and selfish, no one is forcing them to belong to this community. If they want to exclude themselves from the community and its benefits, so be it. God's wisdom allows them to act as they choose. The community respects the individual whom God has made, however mistaken or misled the person may be. As much as the community should pursue and teach God's wisdom, individuals nevertheless are free to pursue another wisdom. That freedom also is part of the natural order. God forces no one to accept His wisdom against his or her will, and it is not the community's goal to exert any such force. This community will exist for the advantages it offers, and freedom from force or oppression by others is one of those advantages.

EDUCATION

Education is the enemy of poorly designed and oppressive social, political, and economic systems. It is an essential companion of a community that exists and operates by force of reason instead of force of arms. Education is a vital strategy for implementing the vision.

Education for maturing in God's wisdom builds community as well as individuals. It helps people to understand the world and how it works as well as the vision and its implementation. Education serves individuals in relation to each other, the community as a whole, and the world in which we must live. It helps people to understand what is expected of them, appreciate their individual freedoms within the community, and work effectively within the natural context of life so the community can be maintained without degradation.

Education of all kinds—physical, mental, artistic, scientific— promotes the maturity of diverse talents to enhance the community's resources. In developing diverse talents according to abilities, education is not necessarily limited to strict forms found in other social contexts. While almost everyone can benefit from basic formal education, formal education also needs to be supplemented with more individually designed education addressed to more specific talents.

Education and maturity is a life-long process. Like everything else, it is governed by natural standards instead of artificial ones. People need to be respected for who they are and can mature to be. Everyone needs to be free to progress in his or her own direction at his or her own rate without the stigma of failing time or age limitations or any other artificial standard or expectancy. The only measure of success is everyone maturing according to his or her own abilities and talents and, of course, contributing accordingly to the community.

The practical distinction between mature and immature is sometimes critical in understanding some biblical texts. It is important as well not to confuse texts addressed to the limitations of the immature with other texts expressing the community's fully mature understanding and practice according to God's wisdom. Unfortunately, that confusion is common when approaching texts from an idealistic perspective, which often fails to make such practical distinctions.

Texts dealing with the special needs of the immature include Romans 14:1–15:3, and 1 Corinthians 8:4–13 and

10:14–33, wherein Paul explains that mature Christians are free to eat meat yet should refrain from doing so when it is a problem for the less mature. That issue may seem strange to us today, but it posed a problem in New Testament times because in the Roman Empire much of the meat initially had been offered as a sacrifice to a pagan god. Eating that meat generally was considered participating in the worship of that pagan god, which was something no Jew or Christian should do. Paul argued that mature Christians knew that such gods weren't real and therefore weren't worshiping those gods merely by eating meat to nourish themselves. However, he also argued that if immature people saw the mature eat meat, they might think the mature were worshiping other gods and that it was alright for Christians to do so. In that case, it would be better, for the sake of the immature, to refrain from eating the meat.

A more complex example of dealing with immature attitudes has to do with attitudes toward women's role in the church, as mentioned in the previous chapter. Again, the point is to deal positively with the needs of the immature, allowing them to mature. The mature need to forbear for the sake of the immature but not to reduce wisdom taught by the church to that level of immaturity and effectively adopt the human wisdom followed by the immature.

The educational process and criteria for teachers and their decisions seem straightforward and unnecessary to elaborate. The major distinction to be observed is in not adopting artificial standards.

LAW

If everyone automatically understood and unerringly followed the underlying worldview in a mature way and could live accordingly, there would seem to be little need for implementation in the form of law. Of course, people aren't born mature, and the mature don't always act wisely. Everyone can use some more specific guidance.

In the discussion of law, it seems helpful to distinguish different sources and functions of law in this context.

LAW DIRECTLY RELATED TO THE VISION AND WORLDVIEW

One body of law is substantive law addressed to promoting life according to the worldview and vision, and avoiding errors or actions to the contrary. This is law that people would reason and test for themselves based on the worldview and vision if they had the time, experience, opportunity, and maturity to do so. Again, this is objective in process, always subject to refinement of understanding.

By way of illustration, the Ten Commandments derive more or less directly from the worldview and promote the vision. The first two commandments, about having no other gods or images, relate to focusing exclusively on the one and only God, who is not the product of our own imaginations, according to the first two axioms.

The third commandment, about not taking God's name in vain, also is close to the axioms. It is trivialized and unduly narrowed when interpreted to prohibit specific types of language. In its full and proper sense, this commandment requires a person to align his or her will to God's will, his or her wisdom to God's wisdom, instead of invoking God's name in the pursuit of his or her own vain, arrogant, artificial goals and separate wisdom. The latter reverses the worldview and is the primary error of many Christians today in their pursuit of artificial dreams and worlds under the pretext of following God.

Doing good for God's creation, humbly enhancing others' lives according to the objective definition of good, also leads to prohibitions against other acts that are obviously incompatible with that purpose. Incompatible acts include killing, stealing, and adultery.

Considering doing something injurious or detrimental to another person likewise is contrary to trying to live in God's context for life. It is a consideration of a pursuit of arrogant, selfish goals. It is the opposite of goodwill and serves to divide people by an artificially constructed barrier of ill will. Therefore, coveting anything belonging to one's neighbor, for example, is prohibited by another commandment. Mental barriers that divide people in the pursuit of selfishness aren't limited to coveting. See 1 John 3:15: "Any one who hates his brother is a murderer, and you know that no murderer has eternal life abiding in him."

Another commandment requires honoring one's parents. It presumes parents who are part of the community and, as a matter of implementation, initially are responsible for their child's growth and character. The best way to honor our parents in this context is to live up to our potential, maturing as we are able within this community of mutual and reciprocal goodwill.

Another commandment may seem at first to be purely ceremonial. It creates one day a week that is dedicated to God (the Sabbath). Dedication to God focuses on the meaning behind God as Creator and that we need to live in God's world, not our own. The Sabbath offers the opportunity to promote perspective and maturity in God's wisdom.

Note Jesus' assertion in Mark 2:27: "And he said to them,

'The Sabbath was made for man, not man for the Sabbath; so the Son (*sic*) of man is lord even of the Sabbath." (Note that the term "son of man," despite capitalization of son in the RSV, appears to be used in a general sense, referring to mankind generally instead of Jesus. The main reason for this conclusion is that the use of man followed by a parallel use of son of man suggests a relationship of terminology, where son of man has the same or a possibly less connotative status as man. It is a common enough literary device in the Bible (see Job 25:6; Psalms 8:4, 80:17, and 144:3; and Isaiah 51:12). Matthew and Luke also appear to use the term son of man in their texts parallel to Mark's text in much the same way (Matt. 12:1–8; Luke 6:1–5). See Appendix C for further discussion of the term son of man.)

God doesn't need rituals and related practices. People need them to help to orient and educate themselves appropriately. The Sabbath was intended as a special time set aside for maturing in education and orientation in God's wisdom free as practicable from the distracting demands of daily work and chores.

The Sabbath's purpose ultimately was to promote good, not to be good or prevent people from doing good. It existed to serve people's needs, not to be served. Recall that Jesus' supposed violation of the Sabbath law was that he and his disciples fed themselves, as the poor did by plucking grain left in the fields for them according to the Mosaic law (Mark 2:23). See also Leviticus 19:9–10, Deuteronomy 24:19–22, and Exodus 23:10–11. (Because the law, as interpreted, also prohibited the poor from carrying grain from the field, they could not gather what they needed before the Sabbath either.)

Feeding the mind does not require starving the body, and failing to meet the most basic needs is contrary to promoting good as objectively defined. Recall also the next, parallel story of Jesus' healing on the Sabbath as a repetition of this theme (Mark 3:1–6).

The remaining commandment forbids bearing false witness against one's neighbor. It is designed to protect implementation procedures, for example, discipline and dispute resolution discussed later in this chapter. The results of implementation procedures may depend critically on witness testimony. Bearing false witness is prohibited because it is effectively an attempt to manipulate the implementation procedure to promote a subjective human wish in lieu of a pursuit of justice in God's wisdom. Similarly, a violation of law is implicit in any other subjective attempt to abuse or undermine any application of implementation in a way that would defeat justice in God's wisdom. See also the section on law-protecting implementation later in this chapter.

The worldview and vision suggest the possibility of many more laws, of course, but a lengthy enumeration seems unnecessary. The purpose in this part is limited to illustrating how and why law develops from the worldview and vision, not to enumerate laws at length.

Natural Law

Natural law, at least as the term is used in this book, does not derive from the vision. The worldview and vision nevertheless suggest the derivation. On one level, natural law includes the attempt to understand the laws of nature. On that level, it is more of a scientific study than a social one. That scientific study and understanding is critically important, but it is left to the scientist and educator, and does not need to be addressed here. It also may be noted that, because the order is basic to the worldview, that study isn't at the level of implementation.

On another level, however, there is a social aspect to be studied and discovered as well, and it is related to implementation. Natural law also involves the natural consequences of the interaction of the natural order with human behavior. Natural law includes human behavior the natural order encourages and excludes human behavior that the natural order discourages. Again, experience and testing typically will be needed to draw reliable conclusions.

An easy example of included behavior drawn from everyday experience and repeated testing is conduct necessary for any higher species to survive, such as killing plants and animals for food, as noted earlier. Such behavior is an expression of maintaining human life with the necessities of survival. The maintenance of other species is otherwise to be encouraged, not merely in self-interest for the future but primarily as part of the overall effort to do good.

A related example of natural law is self-defense or self-preservation under exigent circumstances in order for someone to protect his or her own life. Another related natural law involves rescuing someone from danger. These examples serve the purpose of preserving and maintaining life, even if the decision may involving saving a life at another's expense.

Although this and other societies almost universally consider self-sacrifice the greater act of love (John 15:13: "Greater love hath no man than this, that a man lay down his life for his friends."), it is also difficult and virtually impossible to criticize anyone who nevertheless acts under motives of self-preservation or the preservation of another victim. Both are life-affirming decisions. Anyone faced with a similar decision might do the same.

Because people are inherently different and some might respond to the same situation differently, it is impossible to say that any decision to save a life is wrong. Resort to any immutable idealism as a way of dictating one course of conduct or another imposes only impossible burdens on people contrary to this community's nature. The better response is to accept the results and move on from there.

Another way that natural law is discovered is through behavior that nature may want to prohibit. It includes specific lessons drawn from experience, whereby nature's reaction to the behavior appears to be disapproval. Disapproval may, for example, be in the form of adverse results, or the risk of them, that inhere as natural consequences of that behavior. God's judgment, in essence, inheres in the act's consequences. Natural laws in that respect might be most easily illustrated by health issues related to risks associated with eating certain foods or contracting or transmitting contagious disease that, in the course of doing good toward others, would be avoided.

Marriage appears to be a more complex example of natural law that derives from trial and error rather than anything suggested directly by the worldview and vision. As an understanding of natural law, marriage has proved to be a useful solution for numerous social issues such as enabling more reliable intimate companionship, channeling sexual desires in a socially beneficial way, dealing with procreation and child rearing, and breaking the chain of sexually transmitted diseases.

In artificial contexts, the natural law of marriage was combined with the artificial idea of the family as a separate economic subunit. Ideas of protecting the family wealth sprang from that, including laws relating to inheritance (primogeniture or otherwise) and the stigma attached to illegitimate children. Although the Old Testament seems to have adopted that economic application and similar artificial ideas of economics, Jesus did not. Creating such an economic subunit is creating an artificial division or barrier. It is inappropriate in a natural context where people are economically dedicated to doing good toward others and serving each other's needs regardless of marital or familial status.

Similarly, marriage becomes a commitment of the community as a whole and not merely a commitment between the couple. The community is expected to support and maintain the marriage rather than do anything to tear it apart.

Within the marriage as well, the partners are expected to do good for each other just as they do with the rest of the community, humbling each other for the other's welfare. An example of the latter is the famous "love chapter" of 1 Corinthians 13, which describes love among all Christians, notwithstanding its common association with marriage. More to the point of marriage, Ephesians 5:21–32 holds up reciprocal Christian love as the example of love between Christian spouses. The dynamics of looking largely to self-interest, which tear marriage apart in artificial contexts, do not apply in this context. Note, for example, the one exception allowing divorce in the New Testament: when a spouse who is not a member of the community wants the divorce (1 Cor. 7:15).

Law Supporting Implementation

Laws supporting institutions and procedures established in implementing the world view and vision are designed to help the institutions and procedures accomplish good. An example is the commandment against perjury or bearing false witness, as discussed above, and other examples include prohibited corruptions such as bribery.

It is important to emphasize in regard to laws supporting institutions and procedures that they always be applied to serve the worldview and vision. They are not designed to protect the means of implementation for their own sake because implementation is only a means to a goal, not a goal of the community.

CEREMONIAL LAW

Ceremonial law is a special variety of implemental law. Some people find ritual more important in their lives than others, but most people benefit from some form of encapsulated, symbolic, and ritualized expression of their beliefs together with observing rites of passage. Ceremonial law helps people to focus not on the ritual but on the way of life to be implemented.

For example, Christian celebration of the Last Supper has numerous practical aspects. In addition to ritually sharing in Jesus' last meal with his disciples, remembering and sharing his goal to bring the kingdom of God to all by following God's wisdom, it also is a symbolic enactment of the communal function of service and the meek receipt of good. It is a celebration of life as God intended in the face of any danger posed by those who exert power and coercion to enforce a human wisdom. It is intended to focus, as Jesus did, on God's wisdom and be dedicated to it. There are many other ways in which the purposes of rituals can be articulated, but it is not the purpose here to discuss them in any more detail.

It is important, however, to make a proper distinction between these rituals and magic or witchcraft. The latter may be divided into three categories, each of which calls for a different response. One is stage magic, or ordinary trickery, which is amusing and has educational value. The only problem is when it remains an illusion or deception that serves to mislead or injure.

The second category involves common concepts of sorcery and witchcraft in making spells, hexes, curses, etc. It represents a corrupt worldview, where people assume the role of creator, and spirits or gods are called on to serve human desires. It is an attempt to bend and subordinate nature and everything in it to subjective human desires and create a form of human wisdom. It's about living in an artificial fantasy instead of the real world. It is not a rational attempt to live within an objectively understood context of the real world, and it is rejected for those reasons.

Unfortunately, the attempt to bend God to do human bidding, such as to invoke God's name to succeed at human-oriented endeavors, is a common errant practice among many Christians. It includes prayers promoting secular pursuits and human wisdom, often masquerading under the so-called power of prayer, and pretending that something has thereby magically changed merely because a ritual was performed. Good ritual, including prayer, ought to serve the purpose of focusing on the proper worldview and God's wisdom. See also the discussion of the commandment against using God's name in vain above.

The third category of sorcery or witchcraft includes necromancy, or communicating with the dead. Objectively, there is nothing to be said in favor of it. Those who practice necromancy often prey on others' ignorance, emotions, and vulnerabilities while offering nothing but false hopes and unhelpful information. It is a distraction from a proper focus.

The classic biblical story has to do with the witch, or medium, of Endor, but it hardly is a favorable view. The medium was consulted by an already misguided King Saul (1 Sam. 28:7), but consulting such a person already was a prohibited abomination (Lev. 19:26, 31 and 20:6, 27, and Deuteronomy 18:10–12), and even Saul had previously acted to ban mediums and wizards (1 Sam. 28:9). Saul was falling further away from God's leadership by resorting to such practices. Immediately after consulting the medium, he went into battle, lost his life and Israel was defeated.

This negative view is repeated elsewhere emphasizing, most importantly, the erroneous focus of those practices. See, for example, Isaiah 8:19: "And when they say to you, 'Consult the mediums and the wizards who chirp and mutter,' should not a people consult their God? Should they consult the dead on behalf of the living?" The focus should be on God's wisdom, not human wisdom, whether the human source be alive or dead.

DIPLOMATIC COURTESY

Diplomatic courtesy is normally considered more relevant to external implementation in the next chapter and will be discussed there, but it is an extension of doing good toward others that characterizes internal implementation.

Diplomatic courtesy includes, for example, the law of hospitality in welcoming and doing good toward all, not merely fellow community members. It is a fundamental respect for and doing good toward others as God's creation despite any disagreement as to philosophy, religion, politics, etc., even if others think of themselves as an enemy.

Breaching the law of hospitality toward strangers seems to have been the major sin of Sodom and Gomorrah, primarily through sexual conduct according to their belief in their city gods and imposing their ways on others. Hospitality to strangers is a major imperative in the New Testament as well. See Hebrews 13:2 (Christians should be hospitable toward strangers), Matthew 10:14–15 (referring to Sodom and

Gomorrah in the context of hospitality shown by others toward Christians), and Matthew 25:35, 43 (hospitality toward Jesus/ Christians as strangers as a criterion for final judgment of non-Christians).

LAW-BREAKING

In this context, the term "law-breaking" refers to failing to live according to the worldview and vision. It is not limited to the violation of any articulated law, nor does it refer to an apparently literal violation of an articulated law by an act that is nevertheless consistent with the worldview.

The first category of strategies to deal with law-breaking involves avoiding circumstances which are more likely to produce law-breaking. One strategy inheres in the natural social order by encouraging good toward our neighbors instead of acting selfishly or otherwise against their interests. It seeks to meet others' needs without requiring or encouraging them to resort to injurious behavior to meet their own needs.

A second strategy to avoid potential law-breaking involves an emphasis on education. Education can help to avoid potential law-breaking in three distinct ways. First, it enhances mature understanding in lieu of reliance on subjective and distracting illusions and the injurious behavior they suggest. Second, the discipline of objective thought helps to reduce the likelihood of being carried away by emotions and engaging in rash behavior. Third, it also can help to avoid repeating past mistakes. We can learn not only from our own mistakes but also from the others' mistakes and the consequences of both.

A third strategy of avoidance is to balance immaturity and the need for growth with protecting others from errors caused by immaturity. People are matched to situations they likely can handle, according to the level of maturity they have shown. The effort doesn't avoid error but minimizes mistakes and their consequences. See also Chapter 8 regarding the testing of people according to their level of maturity.

There are deterrents for adverse behavior only to a limited degree compared with other contexts. Deterrents in this context should not be confused with vengeance or retribution, nor should they be confused with coercion or threats, which often are the nature of deterrents in an artificial context. Instead, deterrents are strategies to help people avoid future errors by making them aware of different kinds of errors and their consequences as well as of the need to remedy those consequences as discussed below under dispute resolution and discipline.

When avoidance strategies are not enough, other strategies are needed to meet the needs resulting from the wrongdoing. Dispute resolution addresses the special needs of the injured and restoring damaged relationships. Discipline addresses the special needs of the wrongdoer, whatever they may be, to help him or her mature and return, if possible, to life according to God's wisdom. In these discussions, note that government does not necessarily become involved until the community needs to act as a single body.

Dispute Resolution

The idea of "an eye for an eye" is ancient and said to be included, for example, in Hammurabi's code dated to about 1760 BCE, centuries before Moses. As applied to punishment or retribution, it served to eliminate resort to unbridled emotional responses to others' wrongs and establish a maximum limit on the amount of revenge to which someone may justly be entitled. However, it serves a different purpose in God's wisdom; it isn't about exacting vengeance.

Most people's view of an eye for an eye is one of vengeance, but there is a more basic and important concept behind it: the natural justice that a wrong creates a debt equal to the harm done. That harm includes emotional as well as more direct physical suffering to the direct victim. It also includes any indirect loss to others.

The question of how to repay the debt is a different issue from the question of its measure. Returning evil for evil, adding injury on injury, resentment on resentment, and divisiveness on divisiveness, may seem emotionally satisfying when someone is not thinking clearly, but those responses are as destructive as the original act. In the larger perspective, they are no more justifiable, despite the emotional, vindictive, and coercive rationales that can be suggested.

Repaying with further injury adds that much more loss and disability to the community without doing anything for the victim except pandering to hateful feelings. Punishing the wrongdoer may offer a deterrent effect, but any obligation of debt repayment, along with discipline in the next section, also will do that without unnecessary oppression and coercion.

In Matthew 5:38–42, for example, Jesus rejects an understanding of an eye for an eye as justification for returning violence for violence, and the general context suggests that the saying is probably meant in circumstances beyond merely internal implementation. Note also Romans 12:19: "'Vengeance is mine, I will repay,' says the Lord." See Deuteronomy 32:35. See also Leviticus 19:18: "You shall not take vengeance or bear any grudge against the sons of your own people, but you shall love your neighbor as yourself; I am the Lord."

The better hope to repay, avoid compounding injury upon injury, and heal the victim and community, and to improve life in general is by repaying the debt with doing good. Again the thrust of doing good is to improve the future, not dwell on a past that cannot be changed or corrected. Retribution only helps a victim by addressing residual subjective emotions. The more complete way to deal with the entire loss is by doing good as needed.

Meeting needs is, of course, the ordinary business of the community. A communal effort in this regard is justified since everyone make mistakes, and errors often are interrelated and may be caused by other circumstances far beyond their immediate cause. In effect, everyone owes everyone else, and paying that debt by doing good is the essence of what the community does. Healing is not only the immediate wrongdoer's responsibility, and it is to everyone's benefit that healing and maturity occur as completely and quickly as possible.

It also is important for all parties involved in the event, and the community in general, as a deterrent or for therapeutic reasons, that the wrongdoer recognize the debt, see what injury a wrong can inflict, and make whatever effort he or she can to heal and repair losses. The wrongdoer especially should be willing to take responsibility for meeting the needs that he or she unnecessarily created, including rebuilding the damaged relationship with victims.

How much the errant individual can do depends on his or her abilities. In most cases, the errant individual alone will never be able to repay a particular debt and can only try by helping to repay others' debts. Recall that there is never any *quid pro quo* in the community in respect to meeting others' needs, and the needs involved in repayment of such a debt are no exception. It is sufficient for healing purposes that needs are met from whatever source, which is always the nature of filling needs within this community.

Although a victim's needs typically include emotional injury, victims don't have the right to exact vengeance. The victim, as a community member, isn't freed from the expectancy of returning good for evil. What the victim gets is healing as much as can be achieved under the circumstances. Forgiving the wrongdoer aids this healing process, especially by allowing the wrongdoer to participate.

One aspect of that healing can be venting outrage verbally toward the wrongdoer if it serves a cathartic and restorative purpose. Listening and sharing the pain one has caused, along with an expression of repentance and goodwill, can be one small part of the wrongdoer's effort to help the victim to begin to heal and restore the fractured relationship.

Intentional injury is, of course, much more serious and raises questions regarding the wrongdoer's trustworthiness and intent to remain in the community. Discipline, discussed below, may require considerable testing of the individual, as discussed in Chapter 8.

The dispute resolution systems are aimed at addressing internal injuries, but a similar attempt to respond to wrongs done by members in respect to injuries caused to people outside of the community is likewise in the community's nature.

In contrast, dispute resolution systems designed by fictional contexts are not well suited for members to resolve internal matters. They employ different procedures and laws, and expect a different resolution, all based on a human wisdom. For example, Paul criticized the members in Corinth who took their disputes to the Roman courts and asked if there was no one wise among them (in God's wisdom) to resolve such matters. To bring lawsuits before outsiders, to be judged by the outside world and its wisdom, was a defeat for them as a viable Christian community (1 Cor. 6:1–8).

DISCIPLINE

The strategy of discipline is different in this community compared with most artificial contexts. Its purpose isn't to punish or exact retribution but to do good. The discussion of dispute resolution already has touched on some ways of meeting a wrongdoer's objective needs when injury is caused to another, for example, by increased understanding of the consequences of his or her actions and exercising mature responsibility in returning to a life of doing good toward others, including those he or she injured.

Discipline involves acknowledging a wrong has been committed but, more importantly, it is recognizing that the wrongdoer who desires to remain in the community needs to mature or heal as well. Healing and helping to mature never is an expression of ill will but objective goodwill. Discipline is calculated to serve the wrongdoer's needs to help restore him or her to a life of doing good.

Helpful criticism is the simplest and least intensive means of discipline. However, it requires maturity by the person offering the criticism, so discipline should generally be left to the more mature. Compare Matthew 7:3–5.

The value of helpful criticism would be lost if not followed. Members need to learn to accept criticism and help in the spirit of goodwill that is intended.

Modern Christians are familiar with Jesus' reference to some of his fellow Jews as hypocrites, but it is a mistake to read the modern pejorative and judgmental meaning of hypocrite into the text. The Greek word for hypocrite meant a stage actor. Jesus used the term metaphorically, referring to people who were, to some extent, living according to a fiction, a human wisdom, in contrast to those who lived the real life

God offered them. The point is to be diligent about reasoning according to God's wisdom.

A disciplinary procedure beginning with helpful criticism, and with increasing levels of effort if the criticism is not heeded, is set forth in Matthew 18:15–17: "If your brother sins against you, go and tell him his fault, between you and him alone. If he listens to you, you have gained your brother. But if he does not listen, take one or two others along with you, that every word may be confirmed by the evidence of two or three witnesses. If he refuses to listen to them, tell it to the church; and if he refuses to listen even to the church, let him be to you as a Gentile and a tax collector."

That procedure need not be the exclusive procedure, especially where significant injury is done and needs healing, but it illustrates one useful way of handling relatively minor offenses. The wrongdoer is given the opportunity to change, but someone who ultimately refuses to live according to God's wisdom has effectively rejected community membership. The ultimate stage of ousting such a person from the community formally recognizes that choice by the wrongdoer.

Matthew 5:23–24 addresses another procedure, this time from the wrongdoer's perspective: "So if you are offering your gift at the altar, and there remember that your brother has something against you, leave your gift there before the altar and go; first be reconciled to your brother, and then come and offer your gift."

Depending upon the circumstances and needs involved, there may be a need for more creative and intense forms of discipline involving education, counseling, and other assistance to enhance the wrongdoer's maturity.

The New Testament speaks of punishment by the church in only a few instances, and there is no reason to believe that it involves anything beyond what is mentioned here, including the dispute resolution discussed above. See 2 Corinthians 2:5–11 and 10:6. Recall Jesus' statement to those about to stone a prostitute John 8:7: "Let him who is without sin among you be the first to throw a stone at her."

Recall also the story of Cain and Abel (see Appendix B). After Cain killed Abel, Cain was afraid that others would take vengeance on him, so God promised to protect Cain and put a mark on him to protect him (Gen. 4:13–15). In that text, vengeance belongs to God, even if He decides not to exact it. Human vengeance isn't necessary (see Lev. 19:18 and Deut. 32:35); the focus is doing good.

The primary focus of disciplinary procedures in a society based on doing good is on the present and future, not on the past. With the emphasis on forgiveness, the focus is on moving forward toward good, from wherever the community and its members are at the time, notwithstanding what has happened in the past. The past can't be changed, only the future. If the wrongdoer is willing to mature, the community has gained a brother or sister.

The wrongdoer always has a choice either to live within the community, do good, accept discipline and the obligation to mature, or instead to have a different life outside the community. Others have the same choice, exercised by whether they forgive and are willing to repair damaged relationships.

The refusal to forgive also is contrary to the community's essential nature. Note Matthew 6:14–15, which explains part of the Lord's Prayer: "For if you forgive men their trespasses, your heavenly Father also will forgive you; but if you do not forgive men their trespasses, neither will your Father forgive your trespasses." A refusal to forgive means willfully putting ourselves outside the community and subjects us to formal recognition of that broken relationship by being excommunicated or ostracized.

Likewise, if a wrongdoer refuses to repent, he or she exhibits an intent to continue rejecting the community's way of life. In such situations, the only thing that can be done is to respect his or her decision and formally to accept it, excommunicating or ostracizing him or her from the community until the wrongdoer is willing to repent and participate properly as a community member. That exclusion also protects the community from someone who desires to live by his or her own rules and treats the person as the outsider he or she has chosen to be.

Hope remains that an ousted person or any other person who leaves the community for whatever reason may eventually see how life is worse outside the community and want to return. Compare, somewhat analogously, the story of the prodigal son in Luke 15:11–32. The person is then welcomed back, with the possible condition that a prior wrongdoer submit to some form of discipline or dispute resolution as an acceptance of the ways of the community.

CHAPTER 7

External Implementation

EXTERNAL IMPLEMENTATION ADDRESSES the interaction of those who live within the natural community with those who live outside it. That boundary is not a matter of exclusivity or artificial differentiation between people. It is not designed to be a physical separation, although the practices of others may require some degree of separation as a practical matter. The difference is worldview and way of life. Several contrasting terms could be used to make the distinction between people, such as "member" and "nonmember" or "believer" and "nonbeliever," but the terms "insider" and "outsider" also work.

The most visible differences between insiders and outsiders are the everyday practical conclusions drawn from their respective contexts. Their judgments and behavior are different, drawn from different foundations and rationales that outsiders don't necessarily understand. Unless there is an understanding that another world or context is the basis for the difference, a person living in a fictional context will think insiders are strange or perhaps naive, idealistic, and foolish.

For those living in a fictional world, their situation may seem real and important. There is much that is real about it. Those adhering to their way of life are real. The efforts and strategies they employ, the institutions they create, and their actions and the consequences are real and affect their lives daily. Their foundations, values, and goals, although existing only in the human imagination, are pursued as if they were real. Their every pursuit, however fictionally based, is a real effort and has real effects requiring real reactions. To them, people who don't see everything the same way and live likewise aren't living in what they consider the real world.

Often, as a matter of their own concept of social maturity and economic self-survival, people living according to their fictional worlds may have abandoned previously held immature and idealistic views only to succumb to pressures and adapt to what everyone else around them does. They may tend to look superficially at those living according to a different way as naive, as they once were. They may arrogantly dismiss such people as idealistic or unrealistic, fanatical or narrowly focused, or too ignorant or immature to think straight or behave normally because of their own presumed parallel experience.

Without effective communication, those who haven't adopted real-world foundations will merely assume that reality is as their fictional world suggests it is. They will see those who follow God's wisdom as unfamiliar, strange, and foreign, uncooperative, nonconformist malcontents who, unlike them, don't "go along to get along." They will view meekness as weakness and goodwill without *quid pro quo* or other motivation of self-interest as naiveté or misguided idealism. They will treat those who do not pursue their subjective, vain goals with contempt, as fools, failures, and deadbeats, like a rich man treats a poor man. They will dishonor what God's wisdom treasures and show contempt for what their human wisdom does not value. They will view those following God's wisdom as turning the world upside down with their talk when, considering the underlying bases of everything, those following artificial worlds live in a fiction and refuse to live in and according to the only real world there is. See Acts 17:6 regarding the outsider's view. Contrast Isaiah 29:16: "You turn things upside down! Shall the potter be regarded as the clay; that the thing made should say to the maker, 'He did not make me'; or the thing formed say of him who formed it, 'He has no understanding?'"

Because of the barrier of understanding when living in different worlds, together with all kinds of other artificial barriers and fictions that human wisdom constructs, outsiders may consider those who follow God's wisdom with suspicion or as an enemy of some sort. They fear what they don't understand and seems unreasonable to their way of thinking.

The insider, real-world resident, or whatever someone pursuing God's wisdom may be called, also will see those who follow human wisdom differently and as mistaken, fanatical, and astray, but otherwise not in the same way that outsiders look back at them. In God's wisdom, all that God has created is good and is no enemy. Others deserve to be respected and treated with goodwill the same as any other part of God's world, and the expansion of good throughout the world requires it. That includes doing good to those who may hate in return.

This is another basis of Jesus' teaching not to return evil for evil but to return good for evil, trying to make everything in the world better rather than worse. It makes no difference whether the evil is done by an outsider or, as addressed earlier, an immature insider. Living maturely in the real world God created requires doing good as we can. Doing otherwise effectively is choosing a fiction and different gods, just as the outsider has done. Doing good is the practical thing to do in God's natural world, even if outsiders do not yet appreciate its purpose and practicality.

The challenge, from the perspective of God's wisdom, is most basically in the fact that outsiders pursue the illusions of artificial worlds whether or not they realize it. The conflict between the worlds therefore is not one of physical or psychological violence against anything God has created. It is not to be resolved by some kind of violence between good and evil. It is a peaceful, educational matter of helping others to understand the critical issues of practical context. Apart from self-defense issues, which regrettably may arise by the aggressive actions of the outsider, it is an intellectual, philosophical, and religious battle that needs to be fought with means appropriate to the task: goodwill, reason, and perspective. See 2 Corinthians 10:3–5: "For though we live in the world we are not carrying on a worldly war, for the weapons of our warfare are not worldly but have divine power to destroy strongholds. We destroy arguments and every proud obstacle to the knowledge of God."

Physical battle imagery is an easy metaphor, but only a metaphor where the conflict is not with people, but with their intellectual and spiritual darkness. See also Ephesians 6:13–16. For example, the infamous battle of Armageddon, despite popular embellishment by those who think according to a human wisdom, never occurs in the Bible as a physical war. The armies of the nations gather, but they are defeated by the mere words of God. See Revelation 16–19. That is the challenge and goal for those who think according to God's wisdom.

This challenge is primarily a job for those possessing a

talent for communication and teaching, not just recitation. It requires a relatively full maturity in God's wisdom. It requires a tested individual, and such testing will be discussed in the next chapter.

The ability to promote understanding begins with a respectful treatment and understanding of the outsider, his or her practical foundations, and his or her pressures and expectations in order to converse and present an argument in a way the outsider can understand and appreciate. It is an educational pursuit, and education begins where the prospective student is and with what the student already understands.

Nurturing the outsider cannot be accomplished by an assault of information they cannot understand or a barrage of arrogance or accusation. The purpose of the effort is not to meet the insider's perceived selfish needs or agenda. It is to meet the outsider's needs with a substance and in a manner that is both helpful and perceived as helpful and offered in goodwill. It is not to be presented as judging the outsider but helping him or her to look honestly at the issues and options, and judge them for himself or herself. It is a delicate balance to try to achieve, and undoubtedly many mistakes will be made, which makes the goodwill of the effort all the more important.

"Bible bashing" may seem to the modern impractical Christian to be useful, but it is counterproductive. Instead of respect and goodwill, it shows arrogance and contempt for others and their intelligence. It invites reciprocal contempt and misunderstanding of and aversion to Christianity with the impression that the Christianity being represented by such an assaulting and insulting strategy is a simplistic, stupid, and ignorant religion that cannot withstand the testing of common conversation, reasoning, and courtesy. The practice of Bible bashing may lead idealistic Christians to think that the contempt they receive in return makes them a martyr, but they are only inciting the response by an irrational strategy designed around their own perceived needs and not designed to meet anyone else's practical needs.

Doing good to the outsider requires the same humility as doing good toward others within the community. Again, that humility is not a function of human status, self-abasement, embarrassment, or lack of dignity, nor is it a function of timidness, indecision, or fear. In the face of possible hate and its consequences, it is hardly cowardly. It is, as within the community, a humility and obedience toward God and the context God created. It is a function of treating everything God has created with respect and dignity, deserving of any good effort we can practicably offer under the circumstances, regardless of the recipients' potential for being misguided by their artificial contexts to act very differently in return.

Doing good toward outsiders in God's wisdom also includes respect for any outsider's choice to reject God or not listen, just as God respects that choice without forcing another on anyone. "He who has ears to hear, let him hear" (Matt. 13:9). Disagreement with their decisions is no reason to alter someone's attitude into one of disrespect or ill will, thereby effectively abandoning God's wisdom for a human wisdom. There will be plenty of people looking for a better way of life.

Nevertheless, the hope from the perspective of those following God's wisdom is eventually to reconcile all people to God's wisdom, becoming at peace with God the Creator and His creation. This peace cannot be achieved by spreading ill will and a human wisdom, but only through goodwill and reason, reconciling people who live in fictional worlds to the natural world and God's wisdom. Compare, in this regard, 2 Corinthians 5:16–20.

From now on, therefore, we regard no one
from a human point of view; even though we
once regarded Christ from a human point of
view, we regard him thus no longer. Therefore,
if any one is in Christ, he is a new creation;
the old has passed away, behold, the new has
come. All this is from God, who through Christ
reconciled us to himself and gave us the ministry
of reconciliation; that is, in Christ God was
reconciling the world to himself, not counting
their trespasses against them, and entrusting us
with the message of reconciliation. So we are
ambassadors for Christ, God making his appeal
through us. We beseech you on behalf of Christ,
be reconciled to God.

The good to be done toward outsiders remains defined
objectively by God's wisdom, not the outsider's human-oriented
conception of good. Having the outsider's welfare at heart
does not mean weakly accepting and submitting blindly to
their dictates or aiding their wishes. It does not mean assisting
outsiders to achieve whatever they may desire according to
their human wisdom. It is instead to continue following God's
wisdom with maturity and helping others to perceive that as
the better way to live, that is, helping others to be reconciled
to God's wisdom. See, for example, Romans 12:2: "Do not be
conformed to his world but be transformed by the renewal of
your mind, that you may prove what is the will of God, what
is good and acceptable and perfect." Of course, "this world"
in that quote is a reference to the Roman Empire in New
Testament times or any other artificial world at any other time
as opposed to the natural world God created.

Because good as objectively defined means responding to natural needs in order for the individual to mature, doing good has as wide an application as there are needs to be met. The ways to persuade depend on the outsider's needs.

The extent that insiders can serve outsider's needs depends considerably on a community effort supporting those individual efforts. The outside world will not, as a rule, support the spread of good or the people who spread it. Its own efforts and institutions are designed for different goals.

The community therefore needs to be in a position to provide that support. It needs to remain healthy community and be what it is intended and designed to be. It needs to be able to practice and realize the benefits of the internal implementation referred to in the previous chapter. Members need to be sustained by each other and to grow in such a context. They need refreshment when worn down, goodwill and encouragement when rejected and dejected, inspiration when intellectually drained, and healing when injured, just as they need daily food.

A certain amount of separation is needed for the community to function effectively without undue interference and distraction. That is not the equivalent, however, of defensively trying to protect members from interference and distraction in all respects and at all times. Although there is great temptation to withdraw and live as separately as possible to protect members from sources of corruption, especially the immature, the community also needs to function to do good in all other respects as well. The function to do good includes the difficult effort to spread good to others throughout the world, enlighten them, and bring them to peace and harmony in God's world, reconciling them to their natural context.

Another of the most visible differences between Old

Testament and New Testament involves a difference in approach to external implementation. Although both the Mosaic vision and the Christian vision have the same origin and speak similarly from the perspective of God's wisdom, the Old Testament tradition also tended to emphasize avoiding outsiders as a way of avoiding contaminating influence. It was more a defensive implementation than a positive plan to change the rest of the world.

Jesus and his followers in the New Testament era, in contrast, emphasized an implementation of goodwill to all and reasons for uniting everyone within the natural context and according to God's wisdom. An active and urgent missionary effort was emphasized.

Spreading good throughout the world, most especially in the form of understanding, needs to be recognized as an urgent need for the welfare of the entire world, including the community. As long as people persist in their illusions, they will have contempt for what is real, and they will persecute and destroy the natural world and this community. The urgency in spreading truth and good and in destroying illusions is for the sake of reason, the survival of the real world, and peace.

The reference to peace here is not merely an absence of wars. In God's wisdom, peace is living without warring against God's natural world by pursuing a human wisdom.

In this missionary effort, it typically will be individual members who interact with other individuals outside of the community on its behalf. There may come a time when the community establishes helpful structures and institutions to aid the effort, but for the present, spreading good is the work only of individuals. The imagery that Christians are ambassadors of their community, the body of Christ, is expressed in 2 Corinthians 5:20, and they remain in that capacity at all times in relation to outsiders, even when persecuted and jailed (Eph. 6:20, Philem. 1:9).

While living among outsiders, the mature insider always pursues God's wisdom within the natural context for life, albeit without the same degree of reciprocal nurturing. He or she never needs to leave the natural context, which is everywhere even if the community isn't everywhere. As stated before, no compromise between the natural world and a fictional world is possible without creating yet another fictional world, so life according to the natural context remains the only option. There is no reason to believe that there ever is anything to be gained by following after a fiction or an illusion. The concept of being in the world (dominant fictional world), but not a part of it, is a theme repeated, for example, in Colossians and 1 John.

This special skill and dedication in the course of interacting with outsiders calls not only for maturity but also for a tested maturity (see the next chapter) that remains true to God's wisdom in all situations. Such a mature, tested member cannot be coerced by the human forces that coerce others to live according to fictions. The oppression with which human wisdom is asserted exists to force compliance, but the mature and tested insider does not submit to and live in fear of people and their artificial constructs. The mature individual knows what is truth and what is illusion, and fears God (that is, obeys God's wisdom) rather than men.

That boldness of conviction should not be confused with stubbornness or arrogance. God's wisdom demands that everyone be treated with respect and goodwill as part of God's creation. That respect extends to a limited respect for the institutions that others have created for themselves. Any obedience to the authorities of human wisdom is nevertheless not because the human authorities demand it but because, and to the extent, that God's wisdom may demand it as a matter of respect and goodwill given to all creation.

That respect and goodwill is, at the same time, not a submission to them and the wisdom they represent. It is a diplomatic courtesy as referred to in the previous chapter. Nevertheless, promoting goodwill diplomatically in God's wisdom does suggest tact in several respects, including following whichever of their laws can be followed consistently with God's wisdom, avoiding those laws and human requirements that deny God and do injury to truth or His creation, and communicating those reasons to those who might otherwise misinterpret their actions.

Any dissension or disobedience to fictional laws is clearly not to be conducted with intent to do anything harmful to anyone, even if it might be mistaken or misrepresented as such by outsiders and their institutions. It is to be conducted in goodwill according to truth and God's wisdom in lieu of following the illusion of a human wisdom.

The New Testament speaks of missionaries' imprisonment and martyrdom for many different reasons, all of which were based in religious and philosophical reasons. None involved doing any physical harm to others or taking up arms against secular authority.

The potential for conflict with outsiders because of different worldviews and wisdoms can arise in many ways, for example, where an insider is employed by an outsider. Someone's occupation outside the community does not necessarily denote what that person is inside the community. See 1 Corinthians 7:20–24: "Every one should remain in the state in which he was called. Were you a slave when called? Never mind. But if you gain your freedom, avail yourself of the opportunity. For he who was called in the Lord as a slave is a freedman of the Lord. Likewise he who was free when called is a slave of Christ. You were bought with a price; do not become slaves of man. So, brother and, in whatever state each was called, there let him remain with God."

Problems also arise when an insider marries an outsider. In the Old Testament, marrying an outsider was allowed but usually frowned on as unwise and fraught with dangers. In the New Testament, such a marriage is viewed as potentially separating families. (Matt. 10:34–39). See also the discussion of marriage and divorce in the previous chapter.

The potential situations for conflicts is endless as is the discussion of specifics, but the basic approach remains the same. The opportunity to spread and manifest good can arise from nearly any situation, even when the world does evil to the insider according to its forms of human wisdom. See Matthew 5:39–45.

> Do not resist one who is evil. But if any one strikes you on the right cheek, turn to him the other also; and if anyone would sue you and take your coat, let him have your cloak as well; and if anyone forces you to go one mile, go with him two miles. Give to him who begs from you, and do not refuse him who would borrow from you. You have heard that it was said, "You shall love your neighbor and hate your enemy." But I say to you, love your enemies and pray for those who persecute you, so that you may be sons of your Father who is in heaven; for he (*sic*) makes his (*sic*) sun rise on the evil and on the good, and sends rain on the just, and on the unjust. For if you love those who love

you, what reward have you? Do not even the tax collectors do the same? And if you salute only your brethren, what more are you doing than others? Do not even the Gentiles do the same? You, therefore, must be perfect, as your heavenly Father is perfect.

In context, these sorts of losses, although personal, can be absorbed because of the entire community's support in filling needs and healing injuries. Note also that the text does not mean that, in not resisting an outsider, the insider should act like the outsider or adopt his or her ways, but quite the opposite. It is meant to illustrate taking every opportunity to act with goodwill and perhaps to persuade the outsider.

The insider therefore presses on despite any opposition or persecution which is, after all, the hallmarks of human wisdom. It is to be expected because of the artificial world in which outsiders live, and that needs to change.

The insider therefore looks forward to and works for the day when everyone will live rationally within God's wisdom, and there will be no more illusions, tyranny, oppression, and persecution. In the meantime we can endure everything knowing that whatever evils befall us today may someday cease for the benefit of all. At that time, the battle of worlds will be won—not a battle of armaments but of understanding, of truth vs. fiction and illusion—a result where God, everyone, and everything wins.

CHAPTER 8

Ancillary Implementation

T HIS BOOK HAS thus far addressed time only in more indirect terms and testing only in respect to our understanding and adaptation to nature. This chapter will extend those topics into other important areas, to wit, testing of individuals and the special intervention of God in history.

NATURAL CONTEXT AND TIME

The original context for testing understanding and adaptation is as natural a context as practicable, free from the influences of artificial systems and worlds. That would tend to be limited to the wilderness. See Appendix A.

The wilderness was the primary proving ground in the Bible, the primary context for major life-changing events. The wilderness is where we can best prepare "the way of the Lord," as distinguished from other ways of living (Isa. 40:3, Matt. 3:3). Moses received his revelation in the wilderness, and the people of Israel spent considerable time being tested in the wilderness before entering the Promised Land. See Deuteronomy 8:2–3: "And you shall remember all the way which the Lord your God has led you these 40 years in the wilderness, that he might humble you, testing you to know what was in your heart, whether you would keep his commandments, or not. And he humbled you and let you hunger and fed you with manna, which you did not know, nor did your fathers know; that he might make you know that man does not live by bread alone, but that man lives by everything that proceeds out of the mouth of the Lord." Jesus makes a similar statement when tested in the wilderness (Matt. 4:4).

The gist is that people have life by living within and according to God's creation—"everything that proceeds from the mouth of the Lord," referring to God creating by speaking (Gen. 1). It is to be contrasted to subjective human wisdom, which arrogantly sets up its own context and treats the natural environment only as a resource (bread) to consume.

Before Jesus began his ministry, he spent time in the wilderness being put to the test (Matt. 4:1–11; Mark 1:12–13; Luke 4:1–13). (Note that "Jesus was led up by the Spirit into the wilderness to be tempted by the devil." The text is not an idealistic dualism where the spirit of God is at one extreme and evil at the other. The devil, despite its more common reference to the function to tempt toward a human wisdom, is used in this context to serve a purpose that ultimately serves good. Testing can serve a good purpose when it is not beyond a person's maturity to cope. The Spirit led Jesus to be tempted, analogously to the Israelites being tested by God in the wilderness. Jesus similarly was tested and found to be mature in God's wisdom and therefore prepared for His mission of teaching and preparing the kingdom of God, which proceeded promptly thereafter.)

Human life as a part of that natural context also becomes better understood as the natural community improves in its understanding and adaptation to the natural world. Part of the improvement of the natural community is testing and improving the members.

Testing people in a natural context is analogous to testing people in artificial contexts. It involves two aspects, each relating respectively to the two types of maturity discussed earlier. The maturity that's the focus of this discussion, however, is the maturity in God's wisdom. For the more mature, the more difficult intellectual tests are not those situations where the choice between right and wrong is abundantly clear, although those situations might test character. The more difficult intellectual situations are in the subtleties that cause someone to lose focus and analyze the situation subjectively, not according to God's wisdom. Recall the subtle temptation (or deception) in the Garden of Eden, as discussed in Appendix B.

As with other testing, the wilderness probably is not a practical testing ground for everyone. Substitutes that focus on and test various aspects of maturity in God's wisdom will be needed.

The practice of testing individuals in the past also involved, for example, taking certain oaths of special dedication, such as the Nazirite oath, which could be taken for a period of time or for life (Num. 6). The Nazirite oath involved a strict ritual cleanliness, including avoiding all dead bodies, abstaining from wine and strong drink, and not cutting hair during the oath's term, apparently on the rational that animals in nature do not cut their hair. The practice was meant to bring an individual in touch with God's creation in an especially dedicated, natural, unobstructed, unemotional, circumspect, and non-mind-altered way. Biblical examples of Nazirites include Samson, whose unshorn hair was his strength, yet he appears to have violated the oath more often than not (Judges 13:2).

Interestingly, there seem to be more Nazirites referred to in the New Testament than in the Old Testament. John the Baptist, like Samson, appears to have been a Nazirite for life, dedicated by his parents before birth (Luke 1:13–15; Matt. 11:18). There are ambiguous New Testament texts to suggest that Jesus may have been a Nazirite for a period of time prior to his ministry, though evidently not during his ministry (Matt. 11:19). Note also that Jesus' oath at the Last Supper to refrain from wine until a future time seems to be in the nature of a Nazirite oath (Matt. 26:29). The Nazirite oath also seems to have been a common practice among New Testament Christians (Acts 21:23–24). Although the Nazirite practice may have been helpful to some individuals, it was not itself the community's way of life.

Testing is part of educational growth, not only in terms of measurement of the extent of maturity, but also in terms of promoting maturity. Intense testing is not necessarily good, however, for those who are not yet prepared to withstand the test. Note in the Lord's Prayer the petition not to lead us into temptation (Matt. 6:13). That effectively reminds the community to see to its members' maturity and acquaint them with methods and subtleties of temptation toward a human wisdom. It also reminds them in respect to the community's own testing of members that they should not test candidates prematurely beyond their abilities.

Yielding to temptation and returning to familiar ways of life still can be a problem for those immature in God's wisdom or who have outwardly joined the community for their own motives unrelated to God's wisdom. They may not have a good foundation and, in their superficiality, may not appreciate the difference between reality and illusion, and may become caught up in the illusions once again and go back to them. Note the parable of the sower (Mark 4:3–20). Again, temporarily indulging the immature may be necessary to encourage their greater maturity over time.

To the mature, character in holding fast to God's wisdom isn't so much a matter of stubbornness, special determination, or bravery that others don't possess. It isn't a special innate human power or a human power that needs to be separately cultivated. It is principally the recognition that truth leaves no other viable choice. What is real is real, and what is true is true. For a mature, tested individual, there is no going back to a life based in a fiction. That is the strength of it. No amount of force or violence from those following an illusion can make an illusion seem real once someone sees objective reality. The character is in living according to the truth rather than a fiction.

HISTORY

As part of the natural world, time also merits the effort of objective study in the sense of how God might or might not act in time. History in that respect largely has been ignored in this book but only because of its secondary evidentiary importance, as explained earlier.

Because of God's axiomatic relation to the underlying causal order of the world, we always can assert with objective confidence that God the Creator is always a general, active part of history by acting through the order of nature for the good of the world. It can similarly be asserted that God can work through people who themselves do good. See Romans 8:28: "We know that in everything God works for good with those who love him."

Similarly, the axiom that God is good implies that, if and when God specially intervenes in human history, it is the right time for it to be done. See, for example, Romans 5:6: "At the right time Christ died for the ungodly." God acts in His time, if at all, as He chooses, and it is for humans to accept this and act accordingly if and when they can be identified. Therefore some value can be achieved in an objective effort to try to identify any special interventions of God in human history.

Historians always are trying to learn from history. However, the subject matter and analyses of various historical human actions tend to be as subjective as the pursuit of human wisdom. The focus here, in contrast, is not on a human history or pursuing a human wisdom; it is directed at identifying, if possible, a natural and objective influence on history independent of the influence of humans and human wisdom.

There always has been plenty of subjective anecdotal evidence concerning God's special interventions, and nothing said here is intended to deny that God might intervene in a way that defies objective study. There is no reliable way, however, to distinguish a contention for the latter type of intervention from a flight of the imagination, a misinterpretation of evidence, or any kind of false assertion, either intentional or unintentional. Such an anecdotal study would be, at best, a question of trying to evaluate witness testimony and credibility. If, however, objective study of special interventions of God is possible, it adds a reliability that anecdotal subjective evidence and a finding of credibility cannot offer.

Any special intervention of God in human history would not be subject to objective testing in quite the same way as testing in respect to the ordinary physical context of nature, as discussed in earlier. It is more difficult and has more limitations. For example, the testing must be passive rather than active. Special interventions, as distinguished from God's ordinary interventions through the already established rules of nature are, by definition of the category, beyond any expectation or prediction in the ordinary course of events. They are therefore beyond means of human manipulation or control to produce with any degree of expectation or prediction. We are left to gather what evidence we can, if and when it might occur, without any ability to cause a special intervention by God.

In this respect, the Bible also is not above satirizing others who think they can force or control God to act at our bidding. An example is the story of the prophet Elijah challenging the priests of Baal to a contest to send fire to a sacrificial altar (1 Kings 18:20–40). The priests failed to get Baal to send fire to their altar, whereas God set fire to Elijah's altar despite the altar having been dowsed with water.

This story could be read immaturely as a children's story for its superficial appearance that God reacted to Elijah's bidding while other gods didn't react to their followers' bidding, because those gods don't exist, but a more rational, practical, and mature reading rejects that simplicity. It recognizes that Elijah effectively tricked the followers of Baal using their own ideas of magic and witchcraft against them to demonstrate the error of such beliefs. God's power, as demonstrated by Elijah, was not a special intervention at Elijah's summoning, as it appeared to Baal's followers, who believed in such things. It was God's intervention through the everyday laws of nature. A scientific demonstration of chemically producing fire with the technology and natural materials available to Elijah at the time, consistent with the materials mentioned in the story, already has been made by others. From an objective point of view, the trick criticized those who take a subjective, magical, and superstitious view of the world and try to control it by ritual. That is not to say that God couldn't have intervened specially, but there is no particular reason to believe that God did so in this case, and the story is more meaningful without it.

The inability to force or predict special interventions of God is not to say that they cannot be studied. The objective consideration of testing for such interventions in human history begins as a matter of considering the testing criteria that might be applied. Evidence for this special intervention would have to meet criteria consistent with what we know about God from our observations of nature. Whatever God might do in history would have to be consistent with the axioms identified earlier—not only consistent with God as the Creator of the natural world but also in working to accomplish good, objectively defined, as a result of the event. Otherwise, we could not logically draw any objective conclusion that God the Creator specially intervened in history.

Note that the consistency between God and nature is the reverse of the common subjective misconception that proof of God's intervention in history is through evidence of something unnatural or "supernatural." See also the discussion of subjectively defined religious experiences in Appendix A. God might act outside our current level of understanding, but that is a different question entirely from saying that God acts contrary to or outside of nature. If something is outside our understanding, it is fundamentally illogical to draw any definite conclusions about it. It is imaginatively possible, of course, that God could act in a way inconsistent with the order He created, but there is no particular reason to believe, whether from the Bible or otherwise, that He has ever done so.

God's greatest work, or miracle as it were, is creation itself, and anything created relates to its Creator in the role the Creator made for him or her in the context of creation. Indeed, if God the Creator ever appeared to act contrary to or outside of nature, we would be wisely constrained to redefine our ideas about nature rather than to label any natural event as supernatural.

If the identification of God's special activity can be made in respect to an historical event, it is not necessary to eliminate all other causes as such, any more than it is necessary to find only one cause for any historical event. History generally is a convergence of many different causes. It is sufficient if we can identify if and when God is one of those causes.

Identification criteria might include, analogously to identifying patterns in nature to gain understanding of the underlying laws that govern them, identifying repeated or parallel patterns of historical events. (Analogously, patterns of history may be identified by historians in the effort to learn from the past.) Another criterion would be to satisfy a requirement of nonhuman creation, determining that a pattern works consistently with nature and independently of, or perhaps even contrary to and frustrating, the otherwise controlling human forces at work to promote a human wisdom. Identification criteria also would require these patterns to be consistent with nature's laws and work to accomplish good, as objectively defined, in respect to consequences for human history as well as nature in general. Such criteria may need more refinement to aid the reliability of conclusions, for example, the uniqueness of the pattern or its timing to suggest a special intervention rather than an ordinary intervention through the laws of nature. Other test criteria may be possible, but the purpose here merely is to begin to describe how the effort might be done and not to claim any special expertise in that study. The reason for the study is, of course, to expand possible sources of understanding rather than arrogantly dismiss the effort.

The effort to understand God's influence on human history, for example, by identifying historical patterns, also can lead to something other than a mere chronological view and presentation of human history. Where the focus is to understand God's works and wisdom, instead of the human works and wisdom, it isn't on human history as such.

The identification of objective patterns also would lend itself to comparisons of the historical events falling within the pattern, juxtaposing or superimposing them or otherwise reconciling them to refine understanding of the pattern, just as in identifying physical patterns in nature. The focus is not on a detailed account of human history, but on the historical study of God's work and wisdom so that better lessons can be learned and the pattern might be identified if and when it happens again.

A benefit in gathering and superimposing events is that the attempt can span considerable time and otherwise diverse people, historical contexts, and situations. The more events studied, the more reliable and objective the conclusions potentially will be. A record of such a study would be a source of information unduplicated anywhere else, not as a human history, but as something much more valuable to any purpose to live within the natural world and its history, such as it is. Compiling such a record, or a similar record, is discussed in the next part of this chapter.

Focusing on patterns also may shed light on the role of prophecy and prediction by such a study. The most important role of prophecy would be to identify when and how God is acting in the present. Recognizing patterns identifiable from past experience would add reliability to the understanding. It also would suggest a certain predictability, for example, when a pattern is recognized early enough to suggest its conclusion.

In addition, recognized past patterns also may be used to suggest in a general way how God might be expected to accomplish similar things in the future. Interpreting the present in terms of past understanding therefore would not necessarily be the equivalent of asserting that a past interpretation had suggested specifically what would occur in the future or that anyone in the past was necessarily speaking about the future by expressing his or her understanding. It would be a way of recognizing and pointing to God's activity in the present by recognizing God's activity in terms of similar past identified patterns.

Any objective ability to identify God's special patterns would not necessarily mean that we can go beyond that recognition to suggest more information than a purpose to accomplish good, for example, to suggest a specific motive of God. The importance of appropriately limiting conclusions also is discussed in the Bible, most notably in the book of Job. Job is wisdom literature. That is, it is addressed to the human condition in relation to the context of life. It may or may not have a source in historical events, but the wisdom rather than any human history is the continuing value of the story.

Although the story of Job addresses several other issues and is most commonly cited for a view on human suffering, those are all secondary issues at best. The main focus of the book illustrates the risk of presuming to conclude more from a situation, specifically the issue of God's motives, than we can justly deduce from the evidence, however well-reasoned the explanation may seem.

The book of Job demonstrates this by setting up a background to the human story that is about to unfold. Within that background is a critically important and specific set of motivating circumstances for God, about which the story's human characters will have no direct knowledge. In the tradition of good storytelling, those circumstances are amusing and memorable. God and Satan get into a debate about Job, who is the epitome of a sinless man. Satan argues that Job is a good man because he can afford to be good, because God has made life easy for him. Job is wealthy, loved, and insulated from all manner of harm and difficulties. Satan argues that, if life weren't so easy for him, Job wouldn't be so righteous. God takes an opposing position, and the two make a wager on it. To settle the wager, God allows Job to be put to the test, and the scene then shifts to Job, who quickly loses his family, wealth, and health.

Job experiences the disastrous consequences but has no knowledge of the debate driving the events. Job's friends reason that, because God is just and therefore rewards good and punishes evil, God must be punishing Job for some sin. Job disagrees, correctly because, in addition to what already has been discussed, the story says he had not sinned. However, Job also falls victim to the same narrowly focused rationale. He reasons that he shouldn't be suffering when he hadn't sinned. In his belief that God had been unjust to him Job, in typical human arrogance, demands that God either explain His actions or apologize.

Instead, Job receives God's appropriate criticism, including (Job 38:4): "Where were you when I laid the foundations of the world? Tell me if you have understanding." Job, of course, did not have sufficient knowledge of why he was suffering. He was in no position to know God's reasons or to presume to judge them.

The book of Job then states that, although Job technically never sinned, he nevertheless repented. The repentance was about Job accepting that what God does is good merely because

God does it, without need for explanation and even if, from a human-centered point of view, it doesn't seem fair or just. When Job accepted God's wisdom, he turned away from a human wisdom that presumed to judge God according to an artificial, human-centered worldview and sense of fairness. The book of Job illustrates how making conclusions about God's specific motivations in respect to historical events is risky and always based, at best, on limited information. However rational our reasoning may seem, it is far from certainty to reason backwards from general historical consequences to God's specific motivation or any other conclusions beyond trying to identify if and when God has acted and observing the good result. What God did is a question we might answer. Why God did it is not. The wise thing to do is to adjust whatever God has done, simply because God has done it, just as in adapting to the natural world as the context for life.

Testing of history therefore is to be done with great caution, skepticism, and discipline. It has to be limited to conclusions that can justly be drawn. It is not the primary source of information about life in its natural context in any event. The point, though, is not to trivialize history; it is to appreciate it better in context.

RECORD

The process of learning from testing requires that events, results, and putative conclusions be preserved over time. It avoids having to repeat the same testing every generation or so and allows tests to be repeated accurately if nuances need to be investigated, refining understanding of God's wisdom. It also allows evidence to accumulate for further analysis or refinement in identifying historical patterns.

In an oral tradition preceding a written record, that effort would have required extensive memory and preservation of the wisdom in storytelling, which can encapsulate many nuances within a brief scenario. See Appendix B insofar as it addresses storytelling in an oral tradition in relation to Adam and Eve, and Cain and Abel. Whether oral or written, the purpose is to preserve and build on past wisdom.

In the Judeo-Christian heritage of this discipline, there is sound reason and incentive to record learning, not only about the worldview and vision but also about all kinds of conclusions drawing on them. There is reason to compile, edit, and revise, over centuries of scholarship and testing by diverse experience, everything that may be helpful. This is not only for a more accurate objective understanding of God's creation and how to live accordingly but also for a more accurate objective understanding of how God might also intervene in the course of human history. There is, in short, a practical reason for a Bible. The Bible includes other kinds of related content, of course, but this is the central focus.

Such a practical view of the Bible is as a work in progress, reflecting the objective process, which is a continuing discovery of the natural world and a continuing refinement of understanding. The practical view as a work in progress diverges somewhat from a common modern subjective belief among many Christians that the Bible is the complete and only answer to and conclusion about everything. The latter belief arises out of a subjective approach to understanding, which assumes an ultimate authority, while an objective approach produces the best authority through experience and testing of our natural context, God's creation.

If we look carefully at the Bible, it does not point to itself as anything more than useful for instruction. It is a testimony to

God, His order, and His relationship with creation. It suggests that the ultimate authority for our understanding involves testing everything against God standards, that is, the objective standards of what He has done. Authority is not a matter of subjective human choice or interpretation. That is where humans get into trouble, trying to create their own wisdom.

The need for objectivity to understand God's world makes any record of the attempt to understand it and our life within it a matter of an ongoing objective process instead of any permanently established product of subjective thought or supposedly mystical inspiration. Jesus' emphasis was, like Moses' emphasis, on the worldview and vision that involved this objective discipline and testing.

By Jesus' time, however, there had come to be a general view that prophecy had ceased. The idea that prophecy would have ceased makes sense in terms of a change in focus from an objective worldview and visionary understanding to a focus on a subjective adherence to a tradition of interpreting the law without benefit of the worldview and vision. See the discussion about tradition vs. world view and vision in Chapter 3. There are, of course, similar modern subjective Christian tendencies to want to close the book, so to speak, on additional understanding and to treat the Bible as the end product to be interpreted subjectively rather than as an objective work in progress. Such an attitude is, however, contrary to New Testament teaching.

The New Testament saw a rebirth of the worldview and vision with Jesus and, with it, a rebirth of testing and inspiration. See 1 Thessalonians 5:21–22: "But test everything; hold fast what is good, abstain from every form of evil," and 1 John 4:1–3: "Beloved, do not believe every spirit, but test the spirits to see whether they are of God." The advice in these references was given after Jesus' death, indicating the ongoing process of understanding after Jesus' revelation because of that revelation. The testing refers to testing against God's spirit, that is, the spirit evident in and from God's creation.

All testing against the Spirit was in addition to past testing, to wit, the Jewish scriptures, which is also deemed useful for purposes of instruction. See, for example, 2 Timothy 3:16. It was instructive to the extent it likewise was based on an objective approach and relied on testing against the order God created.

The ultimate authority for everyone should be testing objectively against the reality of the natural world God created, for purposes of orienting life accordingly.

Epilogue

The objective wisdom and natural social order brings practical opportunities to the world and its welfare that have long been missing from subjective wisdoms and fictional worldviews.

There are always many more issues to be discussed, but the purpose of presenting an approach to understanding that is unfamiliar to many people has to be limited to the nature of an introduction to justify the approach. The focus therefore has been on foundations and the more basic conclusions to be drawn from them. This limited focus is especially appropriate where an objective process is advocated. The objective process is not an attempt to present any personal opinion that can extend to every anticipated detail; it relies upon many people over time to improve understanding.

The attempt to show a parallel purpose in the Bible is an expression of opinion, of course, but it is realistic to believe that the Bible would focus on the natural world the Creator created as opposed to systems and worlds of human creation. Living according to the order God established is logically consistent with the manifest purposes of Moses, Jesus, and the Bible, and it has been shown that there is ample reason to believe that the foundations, order, and way of life taught by them basically derives from the effort to adapt to the context for life that God made.

Appendix A:
The Objective Approach

An honest attempt to understand and adapt to the natural world as it is cannot be achieved merely by exercising our imagination or intelligence. It requires more than a reference to widely held beliefs, a pretense that we are emotionally detached, a subjective intent to be objective, and making assumptions about a basic problem that individual human perceptions and ideas begin in our minds as subjective.

The effort requires a disciplined method or procedure designed to produce a reliable objective understanding, notwithstanding human limitations and tendencies to the contrary. The discipline does not have to be developed here because it has already been developed.

The methodology of the discipline is well established and commonly associated with the natural sciences. It often is referred to as the scientific method, but its use is not limited to the natural sciences. It is foundational to this discipline as well because of the goals of this effort to understand the natural world and our best adaptation to it.

The methodology is described briefly here for the convenience of those who may not fully understand or appreciate the discipline. For those familiar with the scientific method, this discussion will not be as important, although there is some value in comments more specifically related to application within this particular discipline. The description of the discipline may be organized or articulated differently elsewhere, but the method is functionally the same.

SUBJECTIVITY

Subjectivity is a limited part of the process. The human imagination is essential, for example, for proposing theories or hypotheses to be tested. An untested theory or hypothesis may be intriguing, but unless it proves reliable, it can't justly be labeled as objective understanding. Rigorous testing against objective standards (those set by nature rather than chosen by us) is key and will be discussed below.

DISCIPLINED OBSERVATIONS

The ability of any observer to make useful observations and gather useful evidence before, during, or after testing starts with disciplining himself or herself to be more objectively minded and avoid subjectivity when making observations. This means the observer should not only familiarize himself or herself with nature and how it works, and how to test things against such standards, but also recognize his or her tendencies toward subjectivity and constantly be self-critical to avoid the influence of one's subjectively preferred observations or conclusions. Self-discipline does not guarantee avoiding subjectivity or making faithfully objective observations, but every effort promotes the objective process.

Useful criticism from others also is part of the process, helping to restrain subjective egos. The reliability of evidence and observations ultimately is verified, not by any standard of relative objectivity of any one observer vs. another but nature's standards. Because those standards do not differ regardless of who observes them, every disciplined objective observer should be able to perceive the same evidence under the same repeatable circumstances.

Consistent Evidence

The requirement of consistent evidence is not an assertion that everything in the world is or must be assumed to be consistent. It is instead recognition that we cannot test our understanding of evidence objectively unless the evidence recurs or repeats consistently.

That consistency applies to observations of test results as well as evidence considered in formulating theories or hypotheses. Unique phenomena that defy explanation beyond speculation and subjective preferences are not yet useful evidence in such a discipline except to suggest a theory to be tested or question an inconsistent theory of understanding.

Unique experiences are unreliable for drawing conclusions

beyond the barest assertion that they occurred. The record of the event is for future reference and consideration in trying to identify a pattern to which like events, if any, belong. The reliability of the historical assertion in turn depends on witness credibility. This is not itself part of the objective process, but a later occurrence of a similar event does lend credibility to the observations. In the meantime, any subjective understanding of the event doesn't thereby become an objective understanding, even if everyone were to agree about it and find it credible. Credibility may offer reason to believe that something happened and it may be very persuasive, but objective understanding must rely on a repeated natural pattern.

It is worth noting that some people refer to unique, especially emotional, experiences as religious experiences. The principal reason seems to have more to do with a subjective understanding and approach to beliefs, whereby the subjective imagination and desires are free to suggest any explanation in support of a person's belief that he or she might be willing to imagine and accept it for whatever subjective reason. Applying the label of religious experience has more to do with the human imagination reacting to the event than with the phenomenon itself, treating religious experience as virtually anything external that has the desired internal subjective response. As such, it is a misnomer as applied to the external experience.

Unique and inexplicable events may naturally fill someone with subjective wonder, set the brain to imagine perhaps an array of explanations that may or may not fit someone's current worldview or scope of understanding, and may often have a profound and lasting impact, but those characteristics are no more reason to categorize the experiences as religious than to categorize them prematurely and subjectively in any other way. The point here isn't to deny either the experience or the impact but to be disciplined in viewing evidence for purposes of the objective method.

Aside from ordinary credibility issues, there also is a question of whether the witness to a unique experience properly interpreted unfamiliar facts or whether, as in some optical illusions, the brain subconsciously and subjectively rearranged the facts to try to make sense of the unusual event in terms of the witness's more familiar or preconceived worldview. For purposes of this discipline, the term religious experience would be more appropriately applied to entirely different types of experiences that have favorably passed objective testing, as will be discussed later in this appendix.

LANGUAGE

Language follows purpose. An objective approach will use different language from a subjective one. A discipline that seeks to answer different questions about the world also will use a different language from other objective disciplines.

As with the sister disciplines of the natural sciences, an important issue with language generally is its inherent limitation that it can express ideas only in terms of other ideas. This presents a risk of either a circularity of logic or, alternatively, a stream of endless definitions unless the language is somehow anchored to and defined by experience of the real, objective world. The language of an objective discipline, including its most fundamental axioms, needs to base its definitions in terms of genuine external experience. Its language also must be as disciplined, precise, and free of subjective usages as practicable. These are, of course, goals as understanding grows, always doing the best we can at any point in time.

Common language is filled with abstract concepts which are useful when descriptive of something natural. If one tries to use language alone to discover or create some kind of so-called "truth," effectively taking abstract categories and absolute concepts out of their natural context, it becomes possible to play games with language to express meaningless concepts. A classic example is the sound of one hand clapping. The resulting expression may be amusing, but it isn't useful to any objective discipline. Language must always be used and understood in its intended context.

At the other extreme of language, objective knowledge, as with subjective knowledge, initially is perceived by the imagination, and it may be perceived before it can be maturely and accurately articulated. Arguably all new objective knowledge and understanding begins that way, independent of the current state of human expression and needing adequate words to be clearly articulated. The natural sciences have addressed new knowledge and understanding by borrowing words from dead languages and redefining them in a way both consistent with the experience and useful to the discipline. In the course of this discipline, to minimize the communication issue, attempts will be made to use familiar modern words as often as practicable, but words will have to take on a meaning appropriate to adapt to the natural context of life.

A parallel situation seems to have been addressed in 1 Corinthians 14:1–19, where speaking in tongues referred to the expression of ideas as yet unable to be communicated to other humans, absent someone else having the ability to translate. As such, it doesn't matter what form speaking in tongues takes, whether in uttering new, previously unknown words or struggling with the inadequacy of someone's common vernacular to express an idea. Its value, if any, is not in the expression of what others perceive only as mindless or incoherent gibberish. It is in the objective reality behind it, begging to be communicated.

REASONING

It is helpful to distinguish two types of reasoning: inductive and deductive. Each has its place, but deductive reasoning is the more reliable and useful method to the objective approach.

Inductive reasoning isn't an altogether invalid way of reasoning. It does bring a sense of order to thought, but it is less precise and inherently more subjective in application than deductive reasoning. Inductive reasoning basically is an attempt to draw one conclusion because another one drawn under similar circumstances seems to be correct. It may infer, for example, that similar evidence requires a similar explanation or conclusion or that similar relationships suggest similar dynamics about the relationships.

That inductive process is more subjective because it involves, at a minimum, a subjective individual judgment of what is similar about different sets of circumstances. Individuals might draw entirely different conclusions based on inductive reasoning. Even if that were not so and everyone thought alike, the inductive process is less precise because there is no fixed conclusions that necessarily follow a given set of facts, as with deductive reasoning.

Any uncertainty doesn't become fatal, of course, unless those conclusions are drawn and accepted without testing, which will be discussed below. Testing is the ultimate and only verification of truth, whether conclusions are suggested either by inductive or deductive reasoning.

When deductive reasoning can be used, it is a more orderly, objective, and preferred way of reasoning. It uses refined rules of logic, deriving conclusions from facts. Specific rules of logic and logical fallacies are discussed adequately elsewhere and need not be repeated here.

The first important use of deductive reasoning is in testing, and that will be explained later. The second important use, which is largely a result of the first, is to deduce more reliable conclusions, provided that the original bases on which the logic operated are reliable. The most foundational of the bases for deductive reasoning commonly are referred to as axioms.

The term "axiom" often is described or defined as a statement that is intuitively or inductively true or that is accepted as true without proof, but these descriptions are inaccurate in an objective context. Axioms may initially be formulated and proposed by intuition, inductive reasoning, or any flight of the imagination, just as with any other hypothesis to be tested, but they become useful only for more objective and deductively logical reasons.

As with other hypotheses, logical deductions drawn from axioms must be verifiable through testing. If their deductions fail testing, the axioms fail, absent some flaw in the testing process or other rational explanation. Axioms, to be treated as such, must always lead deductively to conclusions that, when tested against evidence, not only comport with experience but also demonstrate a superior reliability to conclusions drawn from alternative proposals. If axioms fail to do so and the observations, reasoning, and method of testing are otherwise beyond impeachment, there is reason to question and revise the axioms regardless of however intuitively or inductively true they may initially have seemed to be and regardless of however widely accepted they were before being tested.

Hypotheses

Hypotheses are proposed theories of understanding to be tested for accuracy. The search, of course, is not merely for theories but for those that pass relevant testing such that they can be verified as objective truth. Any hypothesis can be tested for verification or disproof, whether the hypothesis is formulated from deductive logic, inductive reasoning, educated guess, or by a shot in the dark.

Conclusions that have been objectively verified always are subject to later refinement as experience and understanding grows.

Testing

Testing involves comparing experience of nature to whatever a hypothesis directly or deductively implies should be the case if the hypothesis is true. (In a logical either/or situation, testing might alternatively focus on disproving the only logical alternatives.) Testing is distinct from the logical process insofar as logical conclusions also have to pass testing before they may be more than working hypotheses and ultimately accepted as true.

To keep thoughts and convictions oriented and accountable to the real context of life, testing against experience of the natural context of life is essential. A person must be willing to question his or her best ideas rigorously, watch them dissolve and be proven as false, and abandon them when necessary for the sake of objective truth. Testing requires humility, dedication, talent, and intelligence appropriate to the discipline.

Testing is the most important aspect of the disciplinary method. It forces everything about the method, including its axioms and conclusions, to be judged ultimately by the natural world instead of merely by personal subjective judgments, reasoning, or inadequate understanding. Until anything passes testing, it is merely a theory or hypothesis.

The forms of testing can't be described in broad, generalized ways because the range of hypotheses to be tested is theoretically infinite. The procedure needed for any one test depends on the hypothesis and the essential deductive implications to be challenged.

A hypothesis is tested when experiments are designed to expose any flaws in it or its deductive implications. Designing tests can therefore be the most challenging and innovative step of any such discipline.

If the hypothesis withstands every conceivable challenge, it is more formidable, accurate, and persuasive than one that doesn't. Tests designed to challenge a hypothesis, rather than designed to support it, are the hallmark of a genuinely objective discipline.

Tests must be reliable and repeatable. Any other objectively minded and disciplined person who performs the same test should be able to appreciate what is being tested, observe the same results, and draw the same conclusions.

The reliability of such testing also depends on its ability to be logically compelling. In addition to the test being objective and repeatable, the evidence considered must be deductively relevant to the proposition tested. The test must avoid logical fallacies.

One common logical fallacy of those who may consider the possibility of different contexts or ways of life is focusing only on and comparing and criticizing the conclusions drawn from different foundations. It is vital instead to compare their respective foundations. Comparing conclusions while ignoring their different foundations effectively proceeds under the false assumption that the foundations or underlying rationales are the same when they clearly are not and gives a false impression as to the reasoning of either alternative.

Another example is to consider evidence of human behavior. However, the question to be investigated here is not how people might behave if left to their own subjective devices. It is how people should adapt most rationally and effectively to their external natural context in lieu of some internally imagined fiction. When taken out of context and focusing only on human behavior, any kind of human behavior might be considered natural to human behavior, but life in and according to a natural context may demand certain adaptive behavior and reject other behavior. The context is critical.

A related common fallacy is to suggest a theory that children's actions, being less influenced by artificial social structures, would somehow be more naturally correct than corrupted adult actions and therefore that children would live in the most natural way if left alone, free from adult supervision. That theory assumes, however, that natural life is intuitive rather than learned or that wisdom is acquired easily and quickly rather than analyzed carefully and circumspectly over many generations, both of which are obviously contrary to common experience. There also is no reason to believe that children wouldn't need a degree of maturity to survive competently in a natural context, just as they must in any fictionally based context. Children lack good judgment. Children tend to lack not only a sufficient level of experience from which to make circumspect decisions but also the mental capacity to analyze rationally and the discipline to test in any objective way.

Another potential fallacy involves the conditions under which the test will be performed. Testing the understanding of natural life under controlled laboratory conditions, like some natural sciences can do in respect to the answers they seek, has a risk. Imposing limiting, laboratory-type conditions to some extent alters the natural context of life, just as imposing any other artificial context alters it. There is the risk that what has been altered is an influential circumstance, thereby rendering test results illogical and invalid. Someday it may be possible, when a more sophisticated discipline has developed, to account for all the variables affected by controlled conditions in order to produce useful test results. That is not necessarily the present state of the discipline.

The better initial testing conditions would seem to require natural conditions, as best as they can be achieved. The closest thing to the most natural conditions is the natural context of the wilderness. Despite the difficulty of survival in the wild, which also is why it tends to remain relatively natural and free from interference by conflicting human constructs, it is most likely to yield reliable testing results in the natural context of life. Any substitute conditions would have to be considered carefully. Most people obviously won't be able to spend time in the wilderness, and the wilderness may cease to be if they did. Other than the function of testing themselves, most people won't do their own testing anyway.

In circumstances where there are several hypotheses to be tested, and the ability to test them against nature's standards is currently limited by exigencies or unavailable for some reason, a test like Occam's razor might be used as a temporary substitute. Occam's razor involves different rules of thumb. One is that the simplest explanation is preferred over more complex explanations. Another is that the explanation with the fewest assumptions is preferred. There are other rules of thumb as well, but they serve only until the hypotheses can be tested against nature's standards.

Rigorous testing is, as with the sciences, more efficiently performed and taught by those more intelligent and skilled to the objective task. That has several practical advantages in saving unnecessary repetition of testing as well as avoiding poor testing and analyses, and misleading results. Because of the rigorous academic questioning and nature of objective study, an academic effort is preferred, though hardly exclusive. An open mind is always essential.

Of course, we can test only with such understanding as we have. At present, a full and rigorous application of the objective process is frustrated in another respect. Rigorous and specific experimentation also benefits from the experience of a community of people dedicated to such an adaptation, rather than to something else, in order to compare better hypotheses against genuine experience.

We can, however, begin by trying to consider issues in terms of more generalized experience that suggests objectivity from what we know about our natural context from science, for example, or from that which suggests objectivity insofar as certain experience appears to be true invariably in every context of life and the natural context. For those who value the Bible, a related example may include biblical experiences that seem to have involved past experience and testing in an effort to understand of how life is lived in and according to God's created world.

In closing this discussion, it is well to note that there are many scientific theories that have yet to be fully confirmed by testing but serve well as working hypotheses, and there is nothing wrong with treating them as such.

Appendix B:
Adam and Eve, Cain and Abel

ADAM AND EVE

Most people bring some critical misconceptions to the stories of Adam and Eve and Cain and Abel in the book of Genesis. It is worthwhile to consider some of them before addressing these stories and the conclusions to be drawn from them.

First, contrary to the biases of idealistic theologies that many Christians have followed, the Garden of Eden was not an ideal place. There was nothing in Genesis to suggest that it was. It was a garden planted by God and a natural context for human life. It was, in fact, the opposite of any man-made, subjective, artificial ideal of a context for life. It was God's idea of a context for life.

A second common mistake is to presume to read these ancient

stories like they were modern stories. These stories arose from an oral tradition, long before there were any written traditions. Ancient people, even after they could write, didn't have the mass of convenient paper and other writing materials and widespread literacy that we do today. Nearly everything had to be memorized and orally communicated, and finite memory wasn't wasted on trivialities.

With that limitation of memory, the ancients told and retold their most important stories to convey their most important information from generation to generation. This information wasn't dry history or amusing anecdotes; it was their practical wisdom on how to survive.

It was therefore communicated in stories that were memorable, about which they could reflect, discuss, learn, and revise when they had the time. In many ways, these ancient stories became more sophisticated than modern stories. The questions about life that they asked are the same ones we might ask today if we bothered to consider the most basic and important questions in life.

In contrast, in the modern age, where literacy and books are widespread and there's a mass of information at our fingertips, people have been accustomed to more direct messages, less memorization, and less depth of mental reflection. We use different functions of the brain with different degrees of sophistication. We try to absorb huge amounts of information rather than reflect on basic issues, nuances, and contexts. We tend to misperceive biblical stories as if they were modern stories. We tend to look only for direct, superficial, and simplistic messages. We don't expect to have to dig too deep or we expect to be led by the author to consider a deeper question. That isn't the way these stories were constructed.

When modern people think of the story of Adam and Eve from their familiar subjective perspective, they typically think of a rather simple story of two naked people in a garden of fruit trees who disobey God's command not to eat an apple from a specific tree and, as a result, were exiled from the garden and saddle humanity with the problem of sin. Many of the nonsensical modern views about the story aren't in the story at all. The idea that there was an apple, for example, seems to have arisen many centuries after the story was written, when the Bible was first translated into Latin, because the Latin word for sin also was the Latin word for apple. To read the story properly, we need to read the original text carefully and in context.

Considering the context of the story, it may be shocking or scandalous to some people, but the stories of Adam and Eve and of Cain and Abel have two distinct historical contexts, real and suggested. The real historical context of Adam and Eve's story is an era of human history commonly referred to by modern scholars as the Neolithic Revolution. That context is fairly easy to see if we carefully read these stories and know about the Neolithic Revolution. It is the period of time beginning shortly after the end of the last ice age, approximately 12,000 years ago, and extending to approximately 5,500 years ago. During that time, humans left the nomadic hunting and gathering lifestyle to plant crops, domesticate animals, and settle in cities. It is perhaps the most revolutionary change in human lifestyle in the history of mankind.

Like the Neolithic Revolution, the stories of Adam and Eve

and of Cain and Abel begin with life in the garden planted by God, a natural setting, and end with Cain being a farmer or planter of crops who later, in Genesis 4:17, builds a city and, with Abel, a shepherd, one who domesticates animals.

Other biblical information also tends to place the historical context in the Neolithic Revolution. For example, the geographical site of the Garden of Eden is located with reference to the Tigris and Euphrates rivers, where the Neolithic Revolution and the cradle of civilization is considered to have begun. Also, although it seems a bit more of a stretch, the biblical timetable of genealogies following these stories in the book of Genesis places these stories approximately 6,000 years ago, around the end of the Neolithic Revolution.

That era was a time when humans began to change their natural environment for their own benefit on an unprecedented and potentially massive scale. It accordingly suggested profound practical questions about mankind's way of life in relation to the context of nature and the wiser course to follow. These are questions we are asking again today, albeit most often articulated in more scientific terms of environmental issues.

Although the historical context may have raised the basic issues dramatically, and the original version of the story may have initially posed questions in terms of whether the Neolithic Revolution was a good or bad transition, that is not how the issues of the final version are framed. Perhaps after years of reflection, discussion, and debate, the story reframed the issues and answers into a more universal application for all generations, ultimately articulated in terms of Moses' worldview and vision in the text we have. These are issues that have been around since there have been people on the earth.

That more universal application suggests a literary reason for reframing such a story as a wisdom story with a literary context appropriate to its application to all people at all times. It suggests reason to cast the story in terms of the first humans, representing the basic human condition in the world. It is that literary context that modern people most easily see when they read these stories.

Recognition of distinct historical and literary contexts also helps to resolve inconsistencies in the text if we consider only the literary context of the first humans. For example, the historical context explains why other people exist on earth when, according to a strict reading of the literary context of the first people on earth, there aren't supposed to be any other humans on earth. Genesis 4:14 (Cain is afraid that others will find him and kill him like he killed Abel) and 4:17 (Cain suddenly has a wife, who can't be his sister without offending biblical laws against incest.)

As the issues have been framed by the final version of the story, the activities of humans domesticating animals and tilling the soil are within the natural order. They were part of human life before Adam and Eve erred and therefore are not a result of or punishment for the error. See Genesis 1:28 and 2:15.

Building cities is, of course, the natural result of agriculture and being tied to a particular place, and there seems to be no particular criticism of building cities in the stories either. The real underlying issues are not couched in terms of the Neolithic

Revolution but in wisdom issues that are more fundamental and foundational for everyone.

The most basic issue framed in the story's own literary terms relates to the contrast between the fruit of the Tree of Life and the forbidden fruit of the Tree of Knowledge of Good and Evil (Gen. 2:17, 3:3–7). The references to a Tree of Life and a Tree of Knowledge of Good and Evil should suggest, contrary to folklore, that these aren't ordinary fruit trees or even physical trees. They are wisdom trees, metaphors for the wise life and one confused by doing both good and evil. Before Adam and Eve ate of the fruit of the Tree of Knowledge of Good and Evil—that is, experienced both good and evil—everything Adam and Eve had known and experienced in God's completed creation was only good. "And God saw everything that he had made, and behold, it was very good" (Gen. 1:31).

The knowledge of evil is therefore a knowledge or experience of something God did not create, something not part of or consistent with the natural world. It suggests something that mankind created that somehow replaced or obscured what God had created. It is a departure from God's creation to pursue a human creation. It is a use of the human imagination other than for understanding the real world objectively and then using that knowledge in practical accordance with the natural context of life. It is using the human imagination instead to imagine human-defined rules and contexts for life and substituting them for or superimposing them on the real, natural world as a basis for making life's decisions.

That transformation occurred in the story in a subtle way, by a subtle temptation. Adam and Eve were tempted to redefine "good." Instead of understanding good by everything God had done, they included as good what their imaginations perceived as beneficial to human life by using God's creation in a way that He had not intended.

With the knowledge and pursuit of evil as well as good (eating of the Tree of Knowledge of Good and Evil), the pursuit of good alone, as defined by what God had done, was lost. Humans could no longer see reality clearly because their imaginary artificial judgment had created a slightly different worldview and context for their lives, a world superimposed over the real world as a new basis for decision making. Perception changed. Practical judgment was perverted. For example, in Genesis 3:7, after Adam and Eve ate of the fruit of the Tree of Knowledge of Good and Evil, "Then the eyes of both were opened and they knew that they were naked, and they sewed fig leaves together and made themselves aprons." That is not to suggest that clothes are inappropriate or that nudity is the only proper way of life. It instead suggests that any perception by which humans somehow come to be ashamed of, embarrassed by, contemptuous of, or destructive of anything God made is a perception flowing from a man-made illusion.

The statement that their eyes were opened is not to suggest, according to a modern usage, that they were blind before or that it was good that their eyes were opened. It means that they were no longer looking only at the factual truth of nature. They were also looking at something additional, a fiction they created for themselves. It is opening eyes in a negative sense to include something that isn't real but was falsely treated as if it were real. Their eyes were opened to evil as well as to good.

The pursuit of a man-made context for life's decisions also had another inherent natural effect for Adam and Eve and for us.

Insofar as it was a departure from God's context, it alienated them from the garden God had made through the act of obscuring it behind a world of the human imagination. They became unable to live according to the natural order when trying to live according to their own order. God's decision to force them from the garden inhered in their act of pursing an artificial context of life and wisdom. It is the same for us today.

The natural result of no longer living compatibly with the natural world would be that the natural world would no longer seem to cooperate with us. Nature would give the appearance of not working like we would prefer it to work. This is exactly what God's judgment is (Gen. 3:14–19). There are, for example, thorns and thistles—that is, problems dealing with nature— where there weren't any before. Modern ecology could suggest many other examples.

Another way of expressing the same thing is in Genesis 2:17 where, before Adam and Eve ate of the fruit of the Tree of Knowledge of Good and Evil, God indicated that "in the day you eat of it you shall die." When the serpent tempted Eve, it said, "You will not die" (Gen. 3:4). Of course, they didn't die physically in the same day, although mankind ultimately would do so if continuing to live contrary to nature. They did, in any event, die to their relation to God and His creation. They died spiritually, to reality and real life. They no longer lived the life God had made for them, choosing instead to pursue a way of life of their own creation that would not support life like God's creation would.

Instead of recognizing themselves as part of the natural world, Adam and Eve arrogantly imagined themselves as if they were above and apart from it. By creating their own world, they arrogantly presumed to be like God—"You will be like God, knowing good and evil" (Gen. 3:5). They were like God in creating a world for themselves, but that was the problem, not the solution.

The problem is basically one of worldview, of substituting and trying to live according to an artificial worldview instead of a natural worldview. Idealistic interpretations get all of this backwards. Idealism is a subjective process of adopting human-chosen standards, creating artificialities and fictions, and trying to justify everything by those artificial standards. Idealism, as with all subjective thinking, is arrogating our own standards over natural standards. It is the same problem that Adam and Eve had, presuming to be like God, making their own world, and seeing and judging according to human chosen standards instead of accepting God's natural standards and mankind's natural place in the world God created.

"Cursed is the ground because of you" (Gen. 3:17) is ambiguous. It doesn't necessarily mean that God cursed creation. People became a curse on creation by arrogantly choosing to live in a different world of their own creation to the injury of God's natural world. Nevertheless, for the sake of argument, if the curse came from God we need to accept the curse. The result would still be good as understood by what God has done. Either way, we need to accept God's judgment of what our natural context should be. Living according to the order God has made, adapting to nature, would still be wise. Problems arise when mankind tries to do something else.

What we share universally with Adam and Eve is a similar choice. It isn't some kind of imagined concept of original sin whereby individuals are, by nature, sinful—as if anything God has made is somehow not good. The problem that we share over the generations is the arrogant desire to live in the worlds we create for ourselves, in rejection of God and His creation.

CAIN AND ABEL

The story of Cain and Abel presents a variation of the same theme of God's wisdom. As the plot begins to develop, Cain and Abel are trying to be faithful to God, and they choose to show their devotion to Him by voluntarily making a ritual sacrifice, each according to his occupation. Abel the shepherd sacrifices a lamb, while Cain the farmer offers grain. According to the story, God accepts Abel and his offering but not Cain and his offering. Cain becomes jealous and kills Abel. When later asked where Abel is, Cain answers, "Am I my brother's keeper?"

Of course, God knew what had happened and exiled Cain, placing a mark on him. Contrary to many modern views that the mark was a judgment on Cain, the story clearly indicates that the mark was intended to protect Cain from anyone taking vengeance on him for murdering Abel.

There are several curious things about this story. For instance, it does not tell us why God made any distinction between Cain and Abel and their respective sacrifices. Speculators have suggested numerous explanations.

A more popular explanation for God's actions has been to make a distinction between the merits of Cain and Abel's respective sacrifices. Although there is no biblical distinction in worthiness between a grain sacrifice and a meat sacrifice, the text does mention that Abel offered the first or best of what he had, while it makes no mention that Cain did the same. However, that ultimately is not a satisfactory distinction. Sheep are not all the same and there is naturally a first or best one, but the same cannot be said of grain. Grain is not offered by the individual kernel, such that one kernel is distinguishable as somehow qualitatively or quantitatively better than the next. One bulk measure of grain overall is uniform and basically indistinguishable from another unless one measure of grain becomes spoiled or otherwise tainted, but there is no suggestion of that in the story as written. The story doesn't suggest that, in making their respective sacrifices, Cain should have done anything different from what he did or that Abel did anything obviously more worthy than Cain.

Another popular speculation is that God saw something in Cain's character that isn't revealed until Cain kills Abel. However, that explanation effectively reverses the cause and effect of the story as written. According to plot of the story, Cain reacted and killed Abel because God preferred Abel and his offering. The speculation is possible, of course, but that does not appear to be the way the original story was written.

As wisdom literature, it is valid to make any realistic assumptions and argue what effects any additional facts might have in analyzing life's situations. However, any answer based on assumptions added to this story is not necessarily the real point of it as written, and that is what we ought to focus on first.

Efforts to try to infer God's motives may be interesting speculation, but they are more counterproductive than productive to understanding the story as written. For purposes of the story's most basic wisdom, God's motive for making any distinction between Cain and Abel and their respective offerings is unknown, isn't necessary to know, and is better not being known. It is instructive and realistic not to know God's specific motives for anything. That is life. We don't know why the world works the way it does. We can try to understand the rules by which the world works, but we cannot know why these rules and not others. See also the discussion of the book of Job in Chapter 8 regarding presuming to know God's motives.

The more basic problem in understanding the story is worldview. If we look at the story only from the prevailing artificial worldview, we already have elevated our way of thinking above God's way of thinking, and we tend to think that we need to explain God's reasons for distinguishing between Cain and Abel, as if God had to answer to us for His behavior.

That isn't the worldview of the Bible. The biblical worldview is a natural world view, where God's natural world is paramount. We have to adapt to what God has done, whatever that may be, whether or not we fully understand it. God doesn't have to explain His actions according to some artificial human sense of fairness or justice. The story of Cain and Abel isn't meant to explain God's actions in terms of human standards; it is meant to understand people's actions in terms of God's standards.

God's wisdom begins by accepting that what He has done is good for no reason other than that He has done it. Instead of trying to reconcile God's actions to our artificial values, we need to reconcile ourselves and our values to God's actions, whatever they may prove to be, whatever the motives behind them, and however inconvenient or difficult adapting may be. When we don't respond to the reality of the natural world, we have contempt for God and His creation, and we do violence to it, including to each other.

The story illustrates a Cain who had, like many humans have, difficulty accepting God's actions as good merely because God did them. Cain killed Abel because God made a distinction that Cain, applying his own sense of human wisdom concerning fairness and justice, refused to accept. In his effort to reconcile the situation to his own artificial worldview and sense of fairness and justice, Cain committed a great injustice.

Any disagreement or contempt for what God has done, any arrogation of artificial bases for judgment above the basic reality of the natural world is a perversion of perception and leads to violence toward that which is real and good. That replacement of a natural worldview with an artificial worldview was the problem for Adam and Eve and, with a variation in its application, the same basic problem for Cain. They are the same basic problems for us today.

Appendix C:
Jesus

The main part of this book focused on what Jesus taught. This appendix addresses how his followers saw Jesus and his message as a part of the Jewish heritage. As many biblical scholars have noted, Jesus was born a Jew, lived as a Jew, and died as a Jew. His disciples were Jews and, according to New Testament scholars, it is likely that the New Testament writers were Jewish Christians. We cannot hope to understand Jesus without understanding what was most fundamentally a Jewish, or perhaps more accurately, a Mosaic message.

At the more basic levels of worldview and vision, Moses and Jesus seem to have had the same basic focus: the natural world God created rather than any worlds of human creation. Differences between them seem to be limited primarily to the implementation level but, as noted in Chapter 3, the same cannot be said for the differences between Jesus and his contemporary Jews who did not understand his message. The

Greeks and Romans, in contrast, preferred idealistic ways of thinking. The mismatch already has been generally addressed in the main part of the book.

Jesus didn't talk about himself much because his main message wasn't about himself; it was about the kingdom of God. The Gospel of John may at first seem to disagree, but John's focus was more on God's spirit and wisdom, by which Jesus lived and taught, than it is a focus on Jesus as a historical person. For example, while John 14:6 quotes Jesus saying, "I am the way, the truth, and the light; no one comes to the Father but by me," it doesn't take much to understand that this really is a reference to what Jesus taught. Jesus' message revealed the enlightened, nonfictional way to live in God's natural world. Jesus taught the way, truth, and light, not some fiction, and that message is how others can live according to the way, truth, and light. John has referred to Jesus' message in shorthand by referring to Jesus, much the same as we may do today when we reference a specific idea or message by naming a specific philosopher, teacher, politician, or whoever is noted for having championed that idea or message.

Jesus' basic, practical message nevertheless placed him firmly within a long history of teachers, prophets, and other leaders. According to the Gospels, Jesus referred to himself primarily by the designation "Son of Man," indicating how he preferred to think of his own role or purpose within that history.

Jesus' earliest followers taught what Jesus taught, of course, but they also made an effort to express their understanding of Jesus and his message similarly in terms within the same Jewish scriptures and heritage. They came to understand and refer to Jesus as the Messiah, Son of God, and savior, as well as other terms. The titles ascribed to Jesus were Jewish with a Jewish history of usage and definition that Christian theology has long ignored but biblical scholarship is trying to recover.

Unless there was a compelling reason for the New Testament authors to understand the terminology they used differently from the way other Jews at that time understood their own terminology, there is no apparent reason for us to suppose a different understanding of the language used by those authors. They would have wanted their immediate audience to understand what they wrote yet consistently, of course, with what Jesus taught. Their immediate audience consisted originally and mostly of Jewish Christians, together with Gentile Christians who joined the movement later and were learning what was foundationally a Jewish message articulated in Jewish terminology.

Therefore, the only compelling reason to depart from the established Jewish understanding of terminology at that time was if, and only to the extent that, the worldview and visionary understanding taught by Jesus required a different understanding.

Many titles attributed to Jesus do not appear to be affected by the difference between a visionary understanding and the traditional or popular Jewish understanding of that day. One exception is the term messiah (in Greek, *Christos*, or Christ).

MESSIAH

The term messiah in Jewish history could refer to prophet, priest, or king. The term referred to a leader anointed by God.

The greatest role for any messiah is leading the people with wisdom like Moses. That role was set forth in Deuteronomy 18:15–22, the focus of which is in verse 18 where the Lord said to Moses, "I will raise up for them a prophet like you from among their own people." A prophet like Moses was Jesus' function in restoring the worldview and vision essential to understanding the law and allowing people to live with God as their king.

The transfiguration story in the New Testament often is viewed as a mystical experience, but in a practical sense it is one way of explaining that Jesus' disciples recognized for the first time Jesus' proper place in history alongside of Moses and Elijah. That recognition, perhaps even more than the resurrection, solidified confidence in Jesus' message.

It may be helpful to note that there were some differences between the teachings of Moses and Jesus. Most were at the level of implementation. Implementation differences are relatively minor and ultimately matters for testing.

There also seems to have been some influence on Moses, or on those who followed Moses, that did not become part of Jesus' teaching, which students of the Bible may want to consider further. The first had to do with the concept of the Promised Land. Jesus and his followers essentially regarded the Promised Land as the entire earth God made. While that also seems to have been part of Moses' original vision and ultimate goal, the focus somehow shifted to the notion of the Promised Land as the limited geographical area eventually settled by the Israelites.

The second influence on Moses was the twelve tribes who often refused to get along with each other and continued to retain a separate identity from each other. Even later, when King David tried to unite the tribes politically, there continued to be considerable resistance which continued for centuries after that, up to and including the Assyrian conquest, which was the cause for the so-called lost tribes of Israel. The early Christians, in contrast, officially recognized no such tribal or even national divisions. There were only those who pursued the kingdom of God and those who didn't.

The third influence on Moses was the prevailing notion of a patriarchal hierarchy of society. We have no indication that Jesus preached for or against a patriarchal system as such (although the New Testament reports that he taught women as well as men; see also Gal. 3:28). There also may have been a natural basis for some of the practices but, for the most part, it seems to be an artificial distinction to be eventually eliminated.

A fourth influence was the adoption of prevailing economic systems that the people had been familiar with, albeit limited in some ways by the worldview and vision. That also may have been a transitional situation that ultimately never fully evolved as originally intended.

Messiah also referred to the high priest whose function was, in addition to presiding over rituals, to oversee the interpretation and application of Moses' revelation or vision for the entire people. Other than in the book of Hebrews, however, there was relatively little attempt to explain Jesus in such a role.

The role of king is perhaps the most misunderstood of the three roles. When Israel began to have kings, on the rationale that Israel wanted to be more like the other nations (1 Sam. 8:4–5), the term messiah was also used to refer to the king who was chosen and anointed by the high priest.

The introduction of a political king naturally involved transfer of some implementation functions and authority from the priesthood to the king to oversee the people, which justified applying the term messiah to the king. Insofar as it amounted only to a reallocation of duties from one person to another, and the other person was mature enough in ability and God's wisdom to perform the tasks well, it was another form of implementation that was at least functionally compatible with Moses' vision.

The existence of a human king was nevertheless conceptually incompatible with Moses' vision of a nation governed by God as their king. See 1 Samuel 8:4–9, especially verse 7 in respect to establishing a king: "And the Lord said to Samuel, 'Hearken to the voice of the people in all that they say to you; for they have not rejected you, but they have rejected me from being king over them.'"

Having a visible and tangible earthly king, where the real king was supposed to be the invisible and inconceivable God of creation, presented the potential for confusion as to what the nation was about and who was supposed to be in charge. Having an earthly king like other nations paved the way for political revisions and oppressions at the hands of the king like the other nations and for other forms of corruption of the worldview and vision. This included the incidental introduction of pagan religious influences, for example, through royal marriage-based treaties with other nations where the wife maintained her former religion and desired her own place to worship her own gods. Whether or not that marriage was negotiated as part of a peace treaty and seemingly served the people in that way, it also placed the imprimatur of the king on such the corruption by other religions, misleading the people.

Whatever compatibility in practice there may have been under any earthly king depended on the kind of king he was. The biblical measure for whether a king was a good king became a matter of whether the he was humble and pointed to God as the real king (the king of the king or king of kings) and led the people accordingly. If the king pointed to and followed God, the people at least were not misled, and the king's personal immaturity, indiscretions, roughness, and blunders could be more easily overlooked. However, if the king was not humble toward God or pointed to Him as the real king, there were prophets to preach and teach boldly against the king to try to return the people to faithfulness toward God.

By Jesus' time, the Jewish people had been politically dominated for centuries by a series of external empires, with only a few brief periods of self-rule for the Jewish state as a nation. In Jesus' time, the nation was a captive state of the Roman Empire. Rome didn't mind so much what religion or culture any captives followed, as long as they paid the Roman taxes and remained politically loyal to, or at least were not rebellious toward, Rome. Any hint of rebellion was deterred by Rome with as much harshness, cruelty, and humiliation as people could imagine imposing on another person, typically in the form of crucifixion.

Despite the Roman ideas of limited religious freedom, the Jewish state was, from its own perspective, still being subjected to a foreign rule. Roman rule obviously did not point to God as the real king. Jews were in bondage to foreign, unwelcome laws and influences as well as onerous taxes and other oppressions. A hope for a release from that kind of foreign political and military oppression is easy to understand, and it is easy to understand a hope that it might come in a way similar to that of Moses leading the people from bondage in Egypt.

The nature of the Jewish hope for a special messiah by Jesus' time may be difficult to pin down to one concept and may have existed in many forms. Even today, when different people consider the Old Testament criteria, tests, or signs for the promised Messiah, they may refer to different lists of various texts throughout the Old Testament. Those texts typically express some future hope of a better day, a new covenant, world peace, and the like, whereby the present difficulties and troubles are eliminated. Many of the cited texts are associated with the Messiah in the minds of the list makers because of the kind of hope they suggest.

However, the particular list of signs of the Messiah doesn't matter. What people hoped for wasn't necessarily what God's wisdom would suggest. That is a critically important distinction.

In human wisdom, the hope for a messiah was for some great political and military leader who would first defeat the opposition and then, when the leader's military and political authority was sufficiently established, turn beneficently to build a great new government, reestablish the temple, etc.

In God's wisdom, however, the first, and more important, task was to turn people to God's ways, from which the rest would eventually follow. The signs which people look for are all forms of implementation.

If we look at the messianic hope practically and functionally, instead of as a matter of collecting prophetic texts focusing on various accomplishments in the form of implementations, the worldview and vision are foundational and logically must precede implementation. The reverse doesn't work to the same effect because we must build on foundations, not build arbitrarily and look for foundations later. End results, or signs, without people refocusing on the substantive underlying worldview and vision, would amount to empty, superficial accomplishments. There would be little or no substance to the gesture. There would be no real messianic purpose or function at the heart of it, however much it seemed promising superficially.

Focusing on a would-be messiah who would merely perform certain implementation functions as signs misses the mark. A messiah's essential function always was to lead, pointing to God as the real king of creation so people would refocus on and live according to His wisdom. A messiah identified only by performing certain chores as signs, for example, in establishing a political kingship, a territory for that kingship, and the superficial trappings of a religious heritage would have been enthusiastically welcomed, of course, but it would have fallen short of a genuine messianic purpose in God's wisdom.

In applying the title of Messiah to Jesus, his followers were observing the substantive underlying purpose. Christianity has never contended, for example, that Jesus reestablished the Davidic line of kings. That didn't happen and it doesn't matter that it never happened because kings are hardly essential functionaries in a kingdom ruled by God—more the reverse, if the Bible and history generally can teach.

There are several references in the New Testament to Jesus as a king, but they come from the mouths of those who misunderstood him. The gospel of John goes so far as to indicate that Jesus avoided being made a king (John 6:15) and rejected any notion of a kingship in the sense that human wisdom would define it (John 18:33–37), especially "my kingship is not of this world." The closest Jesus came to any claim to the title of king was in entering Jerusalem on a donkey (John 12:14–15), an enactment of Zechariah 9:9–10, which spoke of the arrival of a king of peace. Jesus' role as a king of peace, according to God's wisdom, was to point to God as the real and only king. In God's wisdom, a human king functions to secure God's peace in lieu of achieving some type of military victory or peace sought by human wisdom.

The peace of God is not just any sort of peace or a lack of human conflict as human wisdom would define it. In God's wisdom, His peace involves His creation as He wanted it to be, free of the countervailing forces introduced by human wisdom that wage war against it. God's peace is secured by people abandoning human wisdom and following God's wisdom. Jeremiah 8:8–11 illustrates the same distinction between God's and men's wisdom, and their different concepts of peace: "How can you say, 'We are wise, and the law of the Lord is with us'? But, behold, the false pen of the scribes has made it into a lie. The wise men shall be put to shame, they shall be dismayed and taken; lo, they have rejected the Word of the Lord, and what wisdom is in them? ... from the least to the greatest everyone is greedy for unjust gain; from prophet to priest everyone deals falsely. They have healed the wound of my people lightly, saying, 'Peace, peace,' when there is no peace."

Continuing the discussion of signs of the Messiah, Christians likewise never contended that Jesus reestablished the temple, at least in the sense of a building and the traditional priesthood. However, Christians did claim that the followers of Jesus collectively embodied a temple (1 Cor. 3:16–17 and 6:19), and a priesthood of believers (1 Peter 2:4–5 and 9), and that was in the finest traditions of Moses and the prophets. Exodus 19:6 states, for example, "and you shall be to me a kingdom of priests and a holy nation" See also Jeremiah 31:31–-34:

> "Behold, the days are coming," says the Lord, "when I will make a new covenant with the house of Israel and the house of Judah, not like the covenant which I made with their fathers when I took them out of the land of Egypt, my covenant which they broke, though I was their husband," says the Lord. "But this is the covenant which I will make with the house of Israel after those days," says the Lord: "I will put my law within them, and I will write it upon their hearts; and I will be their God, and they shall be my people. And no longer shall each man teach his neighbor and each his brother, saying, 'Know the Lord,' for they shall all know me, from the least of them to the greatest," says the Lord; "for I will forgive their iniquity, and I will remember their sin no more."

This is realized only by first understanding the worldview and vision before trying to achieve any form of implementation.

Focusing first on the worldview meant that implementation and the so-called signs of a messiah were of secondary importance. Implementation would follow in God's time. See Matthew 12:38–42:

> Then some of the scribes and Pharisees said to him, "Teacher, we wish to see a sign from you." But he answered them, "An evil and adulterous generation [that is, those following human wisdom] seeks a sign … The men of Nineveh will arise at the judgment with this generation and condemn it; for they repented at the preaching of Jonah, and, behold, something greater than Jonah is here. The queen of the South will arise at the judgment with this generation and condemn it; for she came from the ends of the earth to hear the wisdom of Solomon, and, behold, something greater than Solomon is here."

Essentially, although those who sought signs attempted to follow God, they failed to perceive the worldview, and its primacy, effectively failing to follow God. See also Luke 17:20–21. In following their tradition instead, they effectively followed human wisdom instead of God's wisdom. They failed, where others had succeeded, to recognize true wisdom and repent accordingly.

The popular hope in human wisdom for a political/military king/messiah to overthrow the external Roman rule also suffered a separate practical problem in addition to putting implementation purposes ahead of the more foundational worldview and visionary purpose. A political and military solution would have had a remote chance of prevailing at best. In the event of a military confrontation with Rome, there was little doubt which would ultimately have prevailed, absent some special, exodus-type of intervention by God. Any special intervention by God would be His choice, of course, and could not be forced preemptively by human action, such as initiating rebellion. Nevertheless, many tried out of sheer desperation and inability to comprehend an alternative.

The practical problem of facing an overwhelming Roman army was obvious to the Jewish leadership. Insurrection ultimately would lead to a decisive defeat, many deaths, widespread suffering, and utter humiliation for the Jews combined with even greater oppression and fewer privileges under continued Roman rule. It wouldn't seem to be good leadership to pursue such a course of action. Anyone claiming to be a political/military messiah bypassing their leadership and inviting such a disaster was something the leadership rationally did not want.

(Such a disaster occurred only a few decades after Jesus' death when, in 66 AD, a disorganized Jewish rebellion erupted. The result was a bloodbath at the hands of the Roman army and, among other things, the looting and destruction of the temple by the Romans. The military revolt had the reverse effect, in most every way, than what the advocates of a political/military messiah had hoped. The later Bar Kochba revolt, in the early part of the second century, although better organized and more effective in military terms, also ultimately resulted in defeat and additional oppression of the Jewish nation at the hands of Rome.)

There was, however, a more effective way of ultimately defeating foreign oppression than by military action, and it also is more consistent with the underlying messianic vision. It wasn't by trying to defeat Rome by a matchup of military forces; it was through an unanswerable intellectual attack on the fragile, subjective, and unsound foundations of that oppressive way of life. It was educating those who believed in fictional ways to know the truth and bring them within the community of those who followed God.

For that purpose, a fundamentally sound visionary leader, or messiah in its more original sense, was needed, not only for the Jews' liberation but for everyone's liberation from the same misguided and oppressive rule of human wisdom. This gave the Jewish term messiah in its original sense a truly international and universal breadth for all people to share in that hope.

Jesus focused on that more basic and essential messianic purpose of stripping away illusions and reestablishing God's kingdom, whereby all people would live by God's wisdom. It is why Jesus is the Messiah for all people and all people need to recognize it.

Son of Man

Jesus referred to himself as the Son of Man. In the Old Testament, this term referred to a man (or mankind in general) as a son of Adam, that is, as created in contrast to Creator. See Numbers 23:19.

Note that Ezekiel uses that term many times to refer to himself. Daniel also uses the term as a reference to himself, for example, in Daniel 8:17.

The book of Daniel also used the title in association with a special, apocalyptic visionary role. (The term "apocalypse" originally meant a revealing of truth, despite a literary form phrased in visionary and highly symbolic language indicating that the language comes out of a counterculture hiding a message from the dominant culture. Revelation is the intended usage here. It isn't a reference to an epic catastrophe, as the term has come to mean in modern usage.) According to Daniel 7, Daniel had a dream in which he envisioned four terrible beasts, later interpreted as kings of the earth who oppressed people. Their days were numbered because God sat in judgment of them and their dominion was to be taken away by God. Daniel 7:13–14 says, "I saw in the night visions, and behold, with the clouds of heaven there came one like a son of man, and he came to the Ancient of Days and was presented before him. And to him was given dominion and glory and kingdom, that all peoples, nations, and languages should serve him; his dominion is an everlasting dominion, which shall not pass away, and his kingdom one that shall not be destroyed."

The interpretation of the dream in Daniel 7:27 was "and the kingdom and the dominion and the greatness of the kingdoms under the whole heaven shall be given to the people of the saints of the Most High; their kingdom shall be an everlasting kingdom, and all dominions shall serve and obey them."

In this text, someone like a son of man was to lead people to the kingdom of God. The kingdom would be given to the saints, that is, those who followed God and lived in His kingdom. It would eventually replace previous human kingdoms. Recall the gift of dominion in Genesis 1:26.

The function of this son of man was therefore messianic in nature, beginning with a vision of a kingdom of God that was at the heart of Jesus' message. It describes Jesus' intent consistently with his vision and efforts but without the accompanying mistaken popular political/military notions then associated with the title of messiah.

SAVIOR

Jesus' function was reestablishing the rule of God, free from the error, illusions, and oppression of human wisdom. This liberation is why Jesus was, and still is, referred to as "savior." It is a universal message available for everyone.

Jesus is savior in that sense, however, because he carried the message of the kingdom of God and made it available to everyone. In the more ultimate sense, God is the savior. See 1 Timothy 2:3–5 and 4:10.

SON OF GOD

Understanding the background of terms as originally used by New Testament authors perhaps is never more critically important than in respect to the title "son of God." Although most people have tended to understand that term in a Greek or Roman sense, it had a different meaning in the Jewish context, which the New Testament authors understood and used. Unlike Greek and Roman gods, the one God the Jews followed could not be pictured or described. The idea of describing a God who could have children like humans do, as in the Greek and Roman religions, was foreign to a Jewish way of thinking.

The understanding that God is the Creator and the only true God nevertheless lends itself to literary usage of anthropomorphic terms such as "children of God" or "sons of God" in varying levels of meaning. In the broadest sense, just as we may think of things we create metaphorically as our children, even if the creation is inanimate, a similar relationship between creator and created inheres in the act of creating. In that broadest sense, all people and creatures are products of God's order and creation, and can be said to be God's children, regardless of who they are or what they believe or do, merely because they exist. It isn't because they are biologically or spiritually related.

In a narrower sense, those who are true to and follow God are His children in spirit, not merely in terms of physical existence. That spiritual sense is the term's main use in the Bible. On numerous occasions in the Old Testament, the intended relationship of the nation of Israel to God is stated in terms of son to father. See, for example, Exodus 4:22. The Old Testament also refers to the function of the king to be God's son in 2 Samuel 7:13–14. (Note that the title son of God should not to be confused with a different Hebrew term that has been translated into English by the confusingly similar phrase "sons of God," which is a reference to angels, for example, in Genesis 6:2 and Psalm 82.)

The phrases "sons of God," "children of God," and "children of Abraham" are used in the New Testament with the same spiritual sense. See Romans 8:14: "For all who are led by the Spirit of God are sons of God," and Galatians 3:26: "For in Christ Jesus you are all sons of God, through faith." Christians adopted this sense in referring to themselves as sons or children of God. See also Galatians 3:26–27 and John 1:12–13.

In the narrowest sense, the son of God is the ultimate example of one who lives in a spiritually complete, mature way. Such a person is one who is specially dedicated and holy to God. Such a person is the prime example for others to follow, learn from, and try to imitate if they want to be children of God in spirit. It is a reference to an ordinary human being, albeit special and unique in that respect. It is basically in that sense which the New Testament authors refer to Jesus as the Son of God. See also, for example, 1 Corinthians 11:1: "Be imitators of me, as I am of Christ."

Jesus' followers did not refer to him as the Son of God merely because he taught God's wisdom. The title applies because he lived what he taught in an extraordinarily dedicated and exemplary way. Jesus' dedication is nowhere more evident than in the events leading up to His death, where his dedication was tested to the extreme.

Jesus' crucifixion and death need to be understood practically and realistically. It is not a fictional story constructed for idealistic or dualistic theological purposes. It isn't some idealistic battle between good and evil. It is a real story of real people trying to do what they perceived to be right under the circumstances they faced. Most everyone today can understand their motives and identify with any of them if we take the time.

The tragedy in the story isn't that anyone consciously intended to do evil. The tragedy is instead that, in following human wisdom, people acted as their fictions dictated and failed to comprehend and follow God's wisdom. Note 1 Corinthians 2:6–8, especially 2:8: "None of the rulers of this age understood this; for if they had they would not have crucified the Lord of glory."

Jesus' motive in going to Jerusalem apparently was not only to celebrate the Passover but also to communicate his natural vision of God's kingdom to the Jewish leaders who, if they could be persuaded, were in the best position to contribute most to its fruition. Passover also was a time when the Jewish might be most receptive to what was basically a repetition of Moses' liberating message. At the very least, Jesus was driven to try to confront them and present his arguments.

Jesus' actions from his arrival in Jerusalem appear to have been calculated to attract the attention of the Jewish leaders. These actions began with a conspicuous method of arrival, which was an overt allusion to prophecy, and included overturning the moneychangers' tables in the temple.

As a side note, contrary to some suggestions, Jesus did not oppose commerce in the temple. The fact that commerce occurred at the temple violated no law and helped people obey the law. Jesus' teachings promoted keeping the law and commerce consistent with God's wisdom. The idea that economics should be part of and influenced by the practice of their religion was, in fact, a good thing that Jesus otherwise seems to have approved and encouraged.

Jesus' explanation for his actions at the temple was that "you have made it a den of robbers" (Matt. 21:12–13; Luke 19:46). Regardless of the form or forms of robbery, the temple should have been an exemplary place for prayer and focusing on doing good, rejecting influences of human wisdom, and living according to God's order.

Jesus' actions therefore were more than a symbolic act designed to incite anger. It was a categorical rejection of corrupt practices that presumed to place God's approval on misguided human desires and ambitions to the injury of others, contrary to the purpose of the temple and its religious foundations. Jesus' actions supported the temple's function to serve the worldview and vision.

The kind of confrontation with the Jewish leaders that Jesus needed, however, was an intellectual discussion in a forum where the parties were free to argue the merits of their differences, a forum where reason could prevail. Jesus may have been successful in the past when in similar situations while preaching in the synagogues. See, for example, Matthew 12:9 and 13:54, and John 18:19–21. See also Luke 2:41–51, where Jesus, as a twelve-year-old child, conversed freely with teachers in the temple. However, that didn't happen this time.

According to the Gospels, Judas seems to have uniquely and impatiently latched on to the idea that a confrontation with the Jewish leaders could be forced by submitting Jesus to trial under Jewish law, whereby he might present his defense and message. Jesus' disruptive actions in the temple may have seemed to have invited such a scenario. Then, as the reasoning may have gone, Jesus would, at worst, be mildly disciplined for the temple incident and then be free to teach again because he had done nothing seriously wrong under Jewish law to merit any greater discipline. In the process, Jesus might have a forum in which to present his defense of his views to the leaders. If that failed, he could try again. In any event, Judas' plan involved handing over Jesus to the Jewish authorities, not to the Roman authorities.

As a side note, as has been emphasized by others, the Greek word translated as "betrayal" in modern Bibles, in respect to Judas' act, would be better translated as a "handing over." This is how that word is translated elsewhere in the New Testament except in reference to Judas.

For what was considered socially responsible under Jewish law, that is, handing over someone suspected of a crime, most likely in relation to the temple incident, Judas was entitled to payment for the public service. The interpretation of handing over as betrayal, however, implies intent to be disloyal to Jesus, but that is clearly neither Judas' motive nor an explanation for his payment. Judas' status as a disciple and friend of Jesus and his reaction when the Jewish leaders turned Jesus over to the Romans, prove this, as did the fact that he turned Jesus over to the Jewish authorities, not to the Roman authorities.

When Judas learned that the Jewish authorities handed Jesus over to the Roman authorities, he violently returned the money and grieved to the point of committing suicide. That is not the conduct of someone who is disloyal. Making a grievous mistake or being easily deceived is not the equivalent of intentional disloyalty. There is no need to read disloyalty into the story when his actions suggest something else.

Note that when John 13:27 states that Satan entered Judas, it isn't saying that Judas became intent on doing battle against good. It is saying that he was deceived and acted accordingly. In the Bible, Satan tests people to see whether they might act contrary to God's wisdom. Satan therefore becomes the personification of a deceiver and a reference to anything or anyone who deceives. Recall, for example, Jesus referring to Peter as Satan when Peter tried to distract Jesus (Matt. 16:23). Judas was deceived primarily insofar as his plan failed to anticipate why the Jewish leaders would subsequently turn

Jesus over to the Roman authorities, but Jesus appears to have been fully aware of that likelihood.

At his Last Supper with his disciples, Jesus seemed to have been fully aware of Judas' plan, yet he was outwardly ambiguous toward it. Although expressing doubt, if not opposition, concerning what Judas would do, he told Judas to carry out his plan quickly and accepted it. By his actions, Jesus accepted whatever would happen, like everything else about his crucifixion and death. Jesus never tried to manipulate people or force a specific result, as human wisdom tries to do and as Judas was trying to do. Part of Jesus' acceptance was, of course, not trying to manipulate or test God either, as he pursued God's wisdom.

This also was consistent with an often-overlooked part of the Last Supper, where Jesus vowed that "I shall not drink again of this fruit of the vine until that day when I drink it new with you in my Father's kingdom" (Matt. 26:29). Whether or not that was specifically a Nazirite oath (Num. 6:13-21), it was an oath showing His dedication to helping to bring about God's kingdom, however God might choose to do so. That meant, however, that actions beyond persuasion and setting an example were God's to make. God's kingdom is not one where people manipulate others or force results on others. It worried Jesus, of course, that he would be subjected to misjudgments, but that was always a risk, and he could not pursue God's wisdom by turning to pursue a human wisdom. He avoided that deception, and his undivided, uncompromised dedication is what makes Jesus the ultimate example for Christians to follow.

That dedication in the face of adversity is summarized in Jesus' subsequent prayer in anticipation of being handed over: "My Father, if it be possible, let this cup pass from me; nevertheless, not as I will, but as thou wilt" (Matt. 26:39). (This also illustrates the principal purpose of prayer: to bring us into harmony with God's will. See also in the Lord's Prayer, "Thy will be done, on earth as it is in heaven" (Matt. 6:10).) As Paul said, "He humbled himself and became obedient unto death, even death on a cross" (Phil 2:8).

The Gospel accounts of Jesus' trials, first before the Jewish leaders and then Pontius Pilate, seem to have been constructed from inference rather than any direct witness among Jesus' followers. That is consistent with his disciples fleeing after Jesus' arrest (Mark 14:50, 66–72; Matt. 26:56, 69–75).

There basically are three sources for inference. One was the disciples' familiarity with Jesus' message. The second was an understanding of the Jewish and Roman leaders' concerns. The third was the events that led up to Jesus' arrest and the events that ensued.

These events included the result of Jesus' trial before the Jewish leaders, which was to turn him over to the Roman authorities. By inference, the Jewish leaders would have had incentive to do so only if Jesus was seen either as a potential rebel against Rome or as disloyal to God. (In the latter case, the Jewish leaders were prohibited by the Romans to carry out a death sentence, which was the punishment for blasphemy under Jewish law.)

Ultimately, of course, only the charge of being a political rebel would have concerned the Romans and merited a death penalty from Pilate. Of the two possible charges in the Jewish trial, the gospel of Mark adopts the blasphemy rational. Matthew and Luke include both reasons, while John favors the political reason.

Jesus' words at the trials are brief and inferred from what he had said elsewhere. In Mark, for example, when the high priest asked Jesus whether he was the Messiah and the Son of God, Jesus answered, "I am; and you will see the son of man seated at the right hand of Power, and coming with the clouds of heaven" (Mark 14:62). The messianic acknowledgment is, of course, in terms alluding to the book of Daniel, in terms of the son of man and coming on clouds. Such a statement is inferred from Jesus commonly referring to himself as the son of man.

The gospel of Mark has the high priest understanding that reference because the high priest responds that Jesus had committed blasphemy. While it was hardly blasphemy to claim to be the Messiah, a son of man, or even a son of God (in the Jewish sense), it generally was considered blasphemy to claim authority from God independent of how the Jewish tradition understood Moses. Claim of authority independent of the traditional understanding of Moses is what that reference implies and is consistent with Jesus' worldview and vision as the authority Jesus had been claiming all along.

The only thing lacking under the circumstances was the time and opportunity for Jesus to explain his understanding rationally as Moses' understanding, thereby rebutting the charge and persuading the leaders as he had apparently hoped. However, the relative positions of accused and judge weren't compatible with free and equal debate on any issue other than the specific charge alleged. In addition, the exigencies of the trial's timing so close to Passover, when the high priests and every Jew were preparing and anticipating it, also tended to foreclose that opportunity.

The political issue also was a compelling reason for the Jewish leaders' actions, and it probably constituted the more exigent circumstances under which the Jewish leaders would justify immediate action in turning Jesus over to the Romans. The political issue was compelling because Passover was about to occur. Passover is a Jewish holiday celebrating Jewish freedom from bondage to Egypt. It was a short connection to seeking freedom from bondage to Rome, which made Passover a particularly sensitive time to look out for those aspiring to be a political/militaristic messiah.

The Jewish leaders no doubt had their fill of the trouble caused by political rebels, particularly would-be political messiahs, and they could only fear what trouble someone claiming to be a messiah might cause in stirring up the people. Roman response to any insurgency would be swift and harsh, and the Jews had no realistic hope to withstand Rome's army. The only way to prevent a tragic bloodbath was to stop the problem before it turned into a wide scale revolt by stopping those making such claims.

Any potential rebel, as almost all fanatics with messianic aspirations at the time were and which Jesus superficially may have seemed to be, was perceived as more of a liability to the people than the asset such rebels claimed for themselves. The Gospel of John, fond of irony, says the high priest, Caiaphas, was willing to sacrifice one man so that many others could live (John 11:50, 18:14. John 11:45–50 indicates that Caiaphas and others were afraid that Jesus would stir up the people. John, though he loved irony and double meanings, made sure that the reader understood that the irony of Caiaphas' statement was not the full story. John followed the statement with a clarification that Jesus died, however, not only for the nation (in a different sense than Caiaphas intended his statement) but for the children of God (John 11:51–52) and in yet a broader sense for the whole world (John 3:16).) To accomplish that political expediency, which involved allegations of a crime against Rome rather than any Jewish offense, the mechanics of a fair Jewish trial were a bothersome impediment, if needed at all.

Turning over a potential political troublemaker to the Roman authorities would therefore, in the minds of the Jewish leaders, have served the better interests of the Jewish people. It also passed the matter on to the Roman authorities to determine whether Jesus was, in fact, a political troublemaker. If the Romans let Jesus go and Jesus later made political trouble, their own duty to Rome had been performed and only the local Roman government could be blamed. That was a rationale that probably was not lost on Pontius Pilate, and he was not someone to take such a risk.

Jesus' message could not have been understood by Pilate in the limited time of the trial, so there was nothing much for Jesus to say. The gospel of Mark states, apparently from that inference, that Jesus remained silent except in response to Pontius Pilate's question whether Jesus was the king of the Jews, to which Jesus replied, "You have said so" (Mark 15:2). That response, of course, is inferred from the inscription Pontius Pilate later had placed on the cross (Mark 15:26), which was Pilate's published statement of the charge against Jesus for which he was being executed.

Matthew adds little to Mark's account. Any direct claim by Jesus to the title of Messiah was made more ambiguous. In addition, the same question and response in respect to Pontius

Pilate's question of whether Jesus was the king of the Jews was added to the trial before the Jewish leaders, who apparently turned Jesus over to the Romans based on that political charge (Matt. 27:11).

Jesus' death demonstrates an extraordinary dedication to a life lived in God's wisdom despite an excruciating death. It also contrasts in a dramatic way the irrationality and cruelty of human wisdom (the cross) with the reason, gentleness, and goodwill of Jesus acting in God's wisdom. It was a death because of those who followed human wisdom in conflict with Jesus' effort to free mankind from such illusions and error.

For those who can't see the truth, who can only perceive things from the perspective of their fictional worlds, Jesus' death on the cross was a crushing defeat. His life was cut short without accomplishing what he wanted. He died in agony, poor, powerless, and humiliated. Except for a few women, he died alone and abandoned by his disciples.

For those who understand God's wisdom, Jesus taught and lived according to the truth instead of according to a fiction. He endured the harsh tyranny that such fictions could impose on others to promote that fiction, yet he did not suffer defeat by abandoning the truth.

Because of Jesus' inspiring life and death, others could be confident that they could live according to the truth without fear of succumbing to the tyranny of like fictions. They could live inspired in the hope that someday truth would ultimately prevail over all fictions, that goodwill toward all would prevail over all tyrannies and oppressions exemplified by the cross, and that the peace of God would be restored to the earth.

Appendix D:
Paul

The Apostle Paul's letters constitute a substantial portion of the New Testament and number among the earliest Christian writings. It is worthwhile to demonstrate how Paul followed the same practical approach, despite his unique way of articulating issues that has caused his writings to be frequently misunderstood.

Although numerous citations to his letters already have been made, a more dedicated effort in following one of Paul's letters from start to finish may help to establish the point. Paul's letter to the Christian church in Rome (the book of Romans) is not his first, but it generally is considered his most theologically complete and important, so it will serve the purpose.

A General Overview of Romans

The purpose for Paul's letter to the church in Rome is not

directly stated in the letter, and there is no universal agreement about why Paul wrote the letter. Unlike Paul's other letters, this one was written to people he probably did not personally know. The church in Rome had been founded by the efforts of other Christian missionaries who had traveled to Rome before Paul.

One of the more popular suggestions for the letter is that Paul's was introducing himself to the church and explaining his theology. However, there are good reasons to reject that suggestion. Paul's introduction of himself is short. He calls himself a servant of Jesus Christ and an apostle and not much else beyond indicating his travel plans. A lesser problem with this theory is that the letter is not formally addressed to the church leadership, as would be expected if it were a letter of introduction.

As for the letter's suggested theological purpose, there is plenty of theology in it, but the letter is not a straightforward and logical progression of theological thought. We might excuse that in a letter that has been dictated (Rom. 16:22), but there is a better explanation for its organization, which will be discussed below.

We may also ask why Paul would feel any need to explain his theology to the Roman Christians when he had no special personal relationship with them and did not intend to develop one. Although Paul stated that he intended to visit the church in Rome, it was only to impart some spiritual gift and mutual encouragement (Rom. 1:11–12) while on his way to Spain (Rom. 15:24). He apparently didn't have a problem with what the leadership was teaching, so what was Paul's purpose for this letter?

One rationale for salvaging the theological treatise theory is that Paul wrote the letter to defend himself against charges others were making— reading "For I am not ashamed of the Gospel" (Rom. 1:16) as evidence of a defense against criticism. The problem is that Paul makes no defense of himself as such in the rest of the letter. Romans 1:16 also seems to have an entirely different purpose, as will be discussed later. It's possible that the letter is a defense, but this rationale is based on little evidence and is unlikely.

The specific purpose of the letter, though not expressly stated, can be inferred from the general content or subject matter, as well as from its style, that is, its manner of approaching, discussing, and concluding arguments. Looking at these aspects generally, there remains room for disagreement, but one explanation seems most likely. Paul's focus in the letter is not on any elementary, straightforward, and persuasive presentation of his theology. His focus wasn't on his issues at all; his focus was on the local church's issues.

The local church in Rome faced a big problem: being split in two. The body of Paul's letter addressed two factions within the church, a Jewish Christian faction and a Gentile Christian faction. Each was proud of its own heritage and contemptuous of the other's, and their disagreements were making enemies of each other and tearing the church in Rome apart along those lines.

Nevertheless, why would Paul address their issues? Why would Paul intrude in a matter that didn't directly concern him? Why try to build on someone else's foundation when it was not his ordinary practice to do so (Rom. 15:20–22)? Paul's letter doesn't indicate that he had any problem with the church leadership or the message being taught. Would he interlope merely because he later planned to pass through Rome on his way to Spain? Hardly. Wouldn't he offend the church leadership and risk making the situation worse by meddling? Then why virtually ignore the local leaders in his letter? A fair inference, which answers these questions, is that the leadership of the local church in Rome had asked him to write the letter.

In respect to the substance of the dispute, Paul was uniquely qualified to speak. He was a Jewish Christian whose mission has been directed principally to Gentiles, and he was the outspoken advocate that Gentiles didn't have to become Jews to be Christians. To both sides, he was a respected leader, outside the local church and leadership, without anything to be gained by either side "winning." Yet he also shared common interests and understanding with both sides. Compare 1 Corinthians 9:20–21: "To the Jews, I became as a Jew … To those outside of the law I became as one outside the law."

In his letter, Paul intuitively, if not by conscious design, took on a role similar to that of a mediator. He did not take the side of either Jew or Gentile, though he empathized with both. In the style of a mediator, he positively addressed both factions together briefly at first and more at length at his conclusion. In between, he addressed each side separately, albeit in a letter that both sides would read, pointing out the weaknesses in their respective positions in the conflict.

Like a mediator, Paul's approach was gentle, friendly, respectful, and tactful. He did not browbeat them into accepting his conclusions. He did remind them, as a mediator might, of potential severe consequences, not only God's judgment, but also of the potential for church discipline for those who arrogantly refused to submit to God's wisdom. But he didn't harp on that negative message. He wanted to lead them to a positive resolution.

Unlike modern mediators, however, Paul wasn't interested in just any kind of settlement between the factions that they might choose as a position of disgruntled compromise. He was interested in a very particular result that the factions were overlooking and that would bring the peace and harmony of a mature Christian community. Paul wanted to direct the factions gently but surely toward that goal. (He concluded his arguments with, for example, "May the God of steadfastness and encouragement grant you to live in such harmony with one another, in accord with Christ Jesus, that together you may with one voice glorify the God and Father of our Lord Jesus Christ" (Rom. 15:5) and "The God of peace be with you all. Amen" (Rom. 15:33).)

Paul's purpose was not to heal their dissension superficially, bringing a formal end to the overt disruption, but to treat the cause of the problem. He intended for them to focus on and seek God's genuine peace and reciprocal goodwill in His wisdom.

To achieve God's peace, Paul's letter to the Roman church addressed a more important and fundamental problem than the obvious, superficial rift between Jewish Christians and Gentile Christians. The heart of the problem from Paul's perspective, and from the perspective of the God's wisdom, was not their focus on their differences. It was what both sides had in common: hanging on to their forms of human wisdom and not letting God's wisdom govern their behavior.

Paul's purpose was to push the factions tactfully to think in terms of God's wisdom instead human wisdom. That was the spirit they received in faith when they became Christians. That was what would guide them toward doing good for each other and living in peace and harmony with those who were once enemies according to their respective human wisdom.

Paul concluded, in Romans 12 and 13, with his own statement of what that result ought to be. This is perhaps the most complete expression of a mature, practical Christian community in Paul's letters, rivaled in eloquence only by the love chapter, 1 Corinthians 13.

A More Detailed Review of Romans

Paul began his letter with a short introduction, blessing, and compliment that the church's faith was well known. He referred in general terms to the gospel that united them and expressed the desire to be with them to offer some spiritual gift to strengthen them (Rom. 1:1–15). He regretted that his eagerness to preach and reap a harvest in Rome, which was as great as his desire to preach anywhere else, hadn't been realized. He had goodwill toward them, and there was no special reason why he hadn't yet been to Rome. Paul wanted to assure the church in Rome that what he had to say to them was meant only in a spirit of goodwill.

Paul then began the body of his argument with a rather startling statement: "For I am not ashamed of the gospel" (Rom. 1:16). A common mistake is to infer that Paul was defending himself, as if someone had insinuated he was ashamed of the gospel. Nowhere in the letter does Paul defend himself or his own views from any particular accusations. The point of this statement is not a defense of Paul or his views.

The statement was intended to evoke a reaction from his readers, the same way it does to Christians today, to assert that they too are not ashamed of the gospel. The point was to put the question to the factions whether they were ashamed of the gospel but not with a direct accusation, because another accusation was the last thing the two sides needed. The statement was a brilliant, subtle, and gentle challenge to his readers to examine whether they were behaving according to some other wisdom, as if ashamed of the gospel.

From the letter's outset, the factions had been challenged to consider whether they genuinely intended to act according to the gospel or whether the gospel was merely something they pretended to believe while acting according to some other wisdom. Paul challenged them to focus on the gospel's mature implications which, as he argues in his letter, are irreconcilably inconsistent with their continued adherence to human wisdom, which produced their arrogance, boastfulness, and divisiveness.

After that mild but well-defined challenge, Paul turned first to address each faction's pre-Christian background. He began with the Gentiles. He argued that the Gentiles had no reason to boast based on their pre-Christian background. Despite the fact that creation bears witness to God (see Chapter 4), the Gentiles did not see what was obvious or act accordingly (Rom. 1:20–21, 32). By instead adopting human subjective values, they foolishly claimed to be wise (Rom. 1:21–23). Instead of worshiping God the Creator, they worshiped what was created (Rom. 1:25). According to that human wisdom, they engaged in all manner of harmful behavior (Rom. 1:24, 26–31). Therefore, the Gentiles had no reason, because of their past or heritage, to boast or pass judgment on others. Indeed, by hanging on to those ways of thinking, they subjected themselves to God's judgment (Rom. 2:1–8).

One way of thinking that Paul included in his list of wickedness—being factious, a result of not obeying the truth—is mentioned for the first time in Romans 2:8. That was a concern throughout the letter, and it, along with all other forms of wickedness, applied both to Jews and Gentile (Rom. 2:9–11).

Paul argued that Jews or Gentiles who sin, with or without the law, will be judged. In other words, all who do not follow God's wisdom fall short. Conversely, those who do what is righteous, with or without the law, are justified. It is those who do good, who keep the law, who are righteous and just before God (Rom. 2:12–16). Therefore, righteousness isn't a matter of nationality, superficial beliefs, or even having the law; it is a matter of doing good in practice. For Paul, good was, of course, defined by God because He established the standards for life. We don't judge God; God judges us. See Romans 3:3–6 and 9:14, 19–21.

Paul argued that the Jews also had no reason to boast, to the exclusion of anyone else, by reason of their pre-Christian background. While they had the advantage of the law, they also inevitably had broken the law (Rom. 2:17–27). The real Jew is the Jew in spirit. It is the one who keeps the law because it is in his spirit to do so, and that is again not a matter of nationality, ritual, or possessing the written law (Rom. 2:25–29).

Paul nevertheless conceded that it was advantageous to be a Jew before Jesus came along. The Jews who recognized and sought to worship and serve God had received His revelations (Rom. 3:1–2). However, God's faithfulness wasn't because the Jews were always faithful, and it wasn't because they had also been unfaithful (Rom. 3:3–8). Ultimately, even the advantage of the law and the revelations were not enough to attain righteousness, for all had sinned and were accountable (Rom. 3:9–19).

In Romans 3:20, Paul stated that no person is justified before God by works of the law. The reason was ambiguously stated, that "through the law comes knowledge of sin." It is important not to interpret either statement too early, however. Paul explained both assertions later on, without ambiguity.

Paul continued in Romans 3:21–22, "But now the righteousness of God has been manifested apart from law, although the law and the prophets bear witness to it, the righteousness of God through faith in Jesus Christ for all who believe." That was, after all, what Christians, including his readers in Rome, understood and believed. Everything from God, including the visionary revelation of Jesus, had come as a free gift to be accepted by faith (Rom. 3:23–26). With that statement, Paul began to address the factions' post-Christian heritage.

As a free gift from God, there was nothing to boast about, nothing by which either Jew or Gentile could claim more merit than the other. Because faith is a reaction to God's grace or favor (accepting what God has done and living according to what He has done instead of according any artificial world we have created) and not a way of earning God's grace or favor (as works of the law claimed to do), there was nothing to boast about by reason of either faction's post-Christian heritage (Rom. 3:27–30).

Of course, since God is God of both Jew and Gentile, both can live by this faith without distinction. This faith doesn't overthrow the law; instead, it upholds the law (Rom. 3:1), again without distinction between Jew and Gentile. Keeping the law is the result of faith, which is a reaction to God's grace. Keeping the law isn't the cause for God's grace, as if it were earned and something to boast about. We need to react properly to God, not to expect God to react favorably to us.

Paul then turned to reinforce this latter argument to the Jewish faction, using traditional Jewish stories. He argued that God's goodwill has never been earned by obeying the law but had always come freely and only needed to be accepted. Paul used the example of Abraham to illustrate his point (Rom. 4:1–8). Abraham's faith in reacting to God's favor reconciled him to God. Keeping the covenant followed from Abraham being reconciled to God and was not a prerequisite for God's goodwill toward Abraham, or toward anyone else.

Note that Paul did not argue that Abraham (or any other descendant of Abraham) did not have to obey the covenant. He accepted that obedience as a natural and essential consequence of Abraham's faith in God.

Paul similarly argued that God's promise to Abraham and his descendants preceded any of the descendants' attempts to keep the law. Therefore, a faith that reacts to whatever God has done or does is the better determinative for those who are (in spirit) sons of Abraham (Rom. 4:12–25).

Jesus' reaction to God's goodwill became the example and path of that faith (Rom. 5:1–2), so we also are enabled to become sons of God (Rom. 8:14) and children of God (Rom. 8:21) by following Jesus' example of faith and, consequently, obedience. That is the messianic message: that in accepting and reacting to what God has done all people can be reconciled to God and brought under God's rule (Rom. 5:3–11). It restored the opportunity for all to live as Adam was intended to have lived (Rom. 5:12–19).

Paul made another remarkable statement at this point of his argument. He asserted, "Law came in, to increase the trespass" (Rom. 5:20). It is remarkable because the law was intended to do the opposite. What happened? In terms used in this book, the error is in focusing on the law instead of its underlying worldview and vision of life, which is genuinely reactive to all that God has done. Focusing on the law therefore misses its real point as an implementation aid and tempts one to focus on the law as an end in itself. The latter led to a view that keeping the law was a means to gain God's favor or goodwill when we have always had God's goodwill. We only need accept it and react appropriately to it.

The difference in perspective in that focus is basically between considering what is good from a human point of view vs. God's perspective. Focusing on keeping the law to please God and receive His blessing is a change of focus to earning what humans consider good for themselves, thereby redefining good as what serves human interests. It is the opposite of accepting in faith and reacting to what God has done as good merely because He did it.

The errant focus on law as a means to achieve righteousness before God in effect led to substituting a human wisdom for God's wisdom, and following human wisdom increases sin. Recall Romans 3:20. This theme is repeated in Romans 9:30–10:3:

What shall we say then? … that Israel who pursued the righteousness which is based on law did not succeed in fulfilling the law. Why? Because they did not pursue it through faith, but as if it were based on works. … Brethren, my heart's desire and prayer to God for them is that they may be saved. I bear them witness that they have a zeal for God, but it is not enlightened. For, being ignorant of the righteousness that comes from God, and seeking to establish a righteousness of their own, they did not submit to God's righteousness. For Christ [submitting to God's righteousness] is the end of the law [as a basis for a human-defined righteousness], that every one who has faith may be justified.

The result of a life of faith is not to ignore the law but to keep and fulfill it because it is a life reactive to the evidence of God's righteousness and wisdom. A life reactive to what God has done in creation is what the law was originally intended to help implement.

This kind of submission to God's righteousness is not an intellectual abstract belief while living and acting according to some other human wisdom, which breaks God's laws. Paul was hardly urging people to reject one human wisdom only to follow another or break God's laws in one way rather than another. His argument was that there is only one way to fulfill the law: by adhering to the righteousness God established instead of trying to establish our own (that is, creating a purely artificial way to live). What is needed is a reaction to the good that God has done, to see what is good from God's perspective instead of from a human one, reacting and living as God intended as revealed through Jesus Christ (Rom. 5:21).

Paul then interrupted his arguments with three additional arguments in support of his point that Christians should not continue to live in sin (Rom. 6:1–14 and 15–23, and 7:1–6.) These arguments are not logically deductive so much as they are arguments based upon a kind of picture, apparently for the sake of those who might understand pictures better.

The first picture argument is the reference to Christians being baptized into Jesus' death (Rom. 6:3–14). The idea of baptism into Jesus' death is mentioned again, though unexplained, in Colossians 2:12 but nowhere else in the New Testament.

Baptism into Jesus' death was not the practical, mainstream way of talking about baptism in the early church. It was considered a symbolic drowning of the old way of life and beginning of a new one in accord with Jesus' life and teaching. See also John 3:3–6. Paul's general reference to being baptized "into Christ Jesus" (Rom. 6:3) and to "put on Christ" (Gal. 3:27; Rom. 13:14) otherwise seems to be in accord with that mainstream idea.

His conclusion here, despite the different argument, is that Christians should consider themselves dead to sin and alive to God (Rom. 6:11), so it doesn't look as if Paul was attempting to establish a new or different doctrine, despite the different picture he presents.

The picture Paul used seems to be based on his picture of the church as the body of Christ. He made similar arguments elsewhere in drawing conclusions from the body of Christ concept. For example, he argued that Christians, as members of the body of Christ, should not have sexual intercourse with prostitutes because that effectively unites Christ with a prostitute (1 Cor. 6:15).

Although the body of Christ imagery supports the correct conclusion, the conclusion derives more logically and directly from living according to God's wisdom. Using the imagery, Paul had to refer to Jesus' resurrection and life after death to reach the conclusion of how Christians ought to live before their own death. It is a difficult argument to reconcile logically, but if it helps some people who aren't as logically driven to draw the correct conclusion, it serves its purpose.

In Romans 6:15–23, Paul made another picture argument based on the concept of slavery. He argued that everyone is, in a sense, a slave of what we genuinely believe. If we believe in God, we are slaves to God. We can no longer live as slaves to any other way.

That picture has some human familiarity and appeal, but it lacks strict logical sense in the God's wisdom. We do, of course, voluntarily serve God by serving his creation, so the slavery argument in that respect isn't so far off, and Jesus used similar terminology, but we aren't slaves as a human wisdom ordinarily defines the term. The master does not oppress the servant. Indeed, in the course of making the slavery argument Paul remarked, "I am speaking in human terms, because of your natural limitations" (Rom. 6:19). The Christian is free of any practice of oppression. See Romans 8:15, "For you did not receive the spirit of slavery to fall back into fear, but you have received the spirit of sonship," and Romans 8:21, "because creation itself will be set free from its bondage to decay and obtain the glorious liberty of the children of God."

In Romans 7:1–6, Paul again argued for freedom from the law by essentially the same picture argument he used in referring to baptism into death. He argued that Christians are dead to sin and the law (as a means of achieving righteousness) and alive to life according to the spirit of God. There is nothing additional to be said about that argument at this point except to remember that, however unpersuasive or illogical it seems, Paul had already made the logical argument skillfully.

Paul then resumed his more logical and forceful arguments. In Romans 7:7–23, he wanted to avoid any implication that he contended that the law itself is sin (Rom. 7:12) and reaffirm that it only had the effect of leading to sin because people were deceived into pursuing it as a means of achieving a human goal. The more someone pursued it as such, the more he or she was led astray. The effort was tainted by the flesh, that is, by a human tradition or wisdom in pursuing distracting subjective human desires. It resulted in a failure to live as God intended.

The only thing that saves us from that dilemma is living according to God's righteousness and wisdom as revealed in Jesus Christ (Rom. 7:24–25). That sets us free from the flesh (human wisdom) and sets our focus on God (Rom. 8:1–8). That brings real life and the peace of God (Rom 8:6, 9–11).

It is important to observe that Paul wasn't against good works any more than he was against the law. He continued to respect the law (Rom. 7:12). See also Romans 3:31: "Do we then overthrow the law by this faith? By no means! On the contrary, we uphold the law."

Living such a life is the natural response to what God has done.

Paul likewise encouraged works of faith as a response to God, for example, in Romans 12.

This agrees with the book of James. For Paul, we are justified by our reaction to God, which is by having faith in what God has done. When living according to God's wisdom, doing good is the way one lives. Failing to live accordingly means putting faith somewhere other than in God (which is what Paul is trying to communicate to the factions). In James, doing good is the evidence of faith and is what justifies us before God. It's a little different terminology addressing the same understanding because it's addressing slightly different practical issues.

Paul's opposition to any assertion of justification by works is not an opposition to good works; it is opposition to the notion in human wisdom that any good works we do earn God's favor, as Paul as a Jew had previously understood was his incentive to keep the law. (The book of James hardly argues against Paul in that respect, despite a slightly different use of terminology. For Paul, faith necessarily involves good works (Romans 12). A life of faith is a life of good works, keeping the law. For Paul, we are justified by that faith. In James, the term "faith" is used a little differently such that it can theoretically include an intellectual belief separate from resulting actions, to which James responds that such a faith without resulting good works is a dead, or meaningless, faith. James argues that we are justified by resulting works, essentially by a living faith. Both are arguing that the purpose is to live life as God intended. Neither is advocating a human wisdom.)

Paul therefore argued that Christians have been called to life in God's wisdom rather than death in human wisdom (the flesh) (Rom. 8:12–13). All who are led by God's spirit are His sons

(Rom. 8:14). It is what will eventually free the world (Rom. 8:15–27). In the meantime, for those who love God and do good, which is what God intended from the beginning of time (Rom. 8:29–30), He works for good with them (Rom. 8:28). So if God is for us what, except illusion and the human pursuit of fictions, is against us (Rom. 8:31–39)?

Paul sympathized emotionally with his fellow Jews because they should have shared in life as children of God (Rom. 9:1–5). However, being children of God isn't merely a matter of biological Jewish descent; it is a matter of living according to God's promises and seeking to live according to His righteousness (Rom. 9:5–10:21). It isn't that God had rejected the Jews; they failed to understand God's wisdom and effectively rejected God (Rom. 11:1–10) because they had substituted a human idea of righteousness for God's wisdom.

Paul then argued that the failure of the non-Christian Jews to grasp the truth was no reason for arrogance by the Gentiles. The Gentiles had become beneficiaries of what was a Jewish legacy (Rom. 11:11–36). If the Jews could miss the mark so could the Gentiles if they became arrogant and lost focus.

Paul therefore urged all the Christians in Rome to avoid the wisdom of men, not to be conformed to "this world" (Rom. 12:1–2). This world is obviously a world controlled by human wisdom, including the Roman Empire, as opposed to God's wisdom. Christians are to focus on and to be transformed to God's will, doing what is good.

Paul urged the members of the church in Rome to set aside their egos and live in harmony with one another, doing good according to their talents and abilities, recognizing the value of others, loving one another with brotherly affection, setting aside arrogance, and doing good even when evil is done to them (Rom. 12:3–21). It is a beautiful expression of practical Christian life.

Following that powerful conclusion is what has become another misunderstood part of the letter, Romans 13:1–7, which begins, "Let every person be subject to the governing authorities. For there is no authority except from God, and those that exist have been instituted by God."

Unfortunately, those verses often are misinterpreted as suggesting obedience to any governing authority, however evil, oppressive, and ungodly. Therefore, it is important to consider the interpretation of this text in some detail.

Context is important for understanding the author's intended meaning, just as it is important in deciding what another language means, modern or ancient, oral or written. Words taken out of context can be misunderstood, so adhering to the proper original context is critical to understanding the original intent. Context, other than worldview that has already been discussed, will be addressed in seven different categories, as follow:

1. The critical terms of 13:1-7: In the original Greek, the words translated as "governing authorities" (*exousiais huperexousais*) in verse 1 and rulers (*archon*), usually a reference to local authorities, in verse 3 are broad terms which, depending on the context, could refer either to secular or religious authorities. For example, *archon* can be either a reference to local secular rulers, such as in Ephesians 6:12, where Christians are clearly in opposition to them, or religious rulers, such as in Acts 3:17, 4:5,

4:8, and 13:27. The word *huperexousias* (apparently indicating higher or the highest authorities in conjunction with *exousias*, translated as "governing" in the RSV) isn't used elsewhere in the New Testament. The specific words are therefore inconclusive by themselves without considering their usage in context.

2. Usage in Paul's other letters: Paul's other writings using the term *exousia* or its variations always refer to spiritual authority, never to secular authority. This suggests a preference for interpreting Romans 13:1–7 as a reference only to church authority, although other interpretations can't yet be ruled out solely on that basis.

Titus 3:1 is a somewhat parallel text to this passage in Romans. Although Paul's authorship of Titus has been debated, the tradition is followed to avoid getting into issues that don't matter much here. For those who nevertheless dispute Paul's authorship, the references and arguments presented here would belong to a different category of context and the net effect of the distinction would be relatively minor.

The book of Titus was a letter written to Titus who was a church leader and had the duty of appointing elders (Titus 1:6) and rebuking those who had been insubordinate and deceptive (Titus 1:10–14). Titus 2:15–3:1 then states, "Declare these things; exhort and reprove with all authority. Let no one disregard you. *Remind them to be submissive to rulers and authorities*, to be obedient, to be ready for any honest work, to speak evil of no one, to avoid quarreling, to be gentle, and to show perfect courtesy to all men" (emphasis added). (Note that the word for authority in the first sentence is from the Greek word transliterated *epitages*, not *exousia*. *Epitages* is also translated as "command" in some other New Testament translations.)

As in Romans, the terms for rulers and authorities used in the emphasized part of this passage from Titus are the plural of *archon* and *exousia*. This is unmistakably an exhortation to Titus to exercise church authority over the members. The theme continues in Titus 3:8–10: "I desire you to insist on these things, so that those who have believed in God may be careful to apply themselves to good deeds; these are excellent and profitable to men. But avoid stupid controversies, genealogies, dissensions, and quarrels over the law, for they are unprofitable and futile. As for a man who is factious, after admonishing him once or twice, have nothing more to do with him, knowing that such a person is perverted and sinful; he is self-condemned."

This book clearly states the intent to refer to church authorities keeping peace and excommunicating stubborn and intentionally divisive people who would not heed church authorities. The problem of divisiveness (and not listening to church authorities) is, of course, common to the book of Romans, as already discussed.

The parallel in Titus is a particularly striking one, but it is not the only parallel reference in Paul's other letters. Church response to division was also addressed, for example, in 1 Corinthians 3, where some arrogantly claimed superiority over others based on who baptized them, that is, who they claimed to "belong to," Paul or Apollos (another Christian missionary) as if who baptized them made a difference.

In 1 Corinthians 4:17–21, Paul warned disruptive ones that he would come either bearing a rod (applying discipline) or with love in a spirit of gentleness. Paul repeated that theme later when he urged them not to despise Timothy (1 Cor. 16:11) and to be subject to those who had worked long and hard to the service of the saints (1 Cor. 16:15–16). The parallels in respect to church divisiveness are too similar to ignore or dismiss as mere coincidence.

The references in Titus and 1 Corinthians are clearly to obedience to church authority and not to secular authority, tending to support a parallel interpretation and application of the Romans text. But there is much more to suggest that interpretation.

3. Literary context within the letter to the Romans: To interpret Romans 13:1–7 to refer to secular authorities is entirely disjunctive and out of place within the letter itself. Every other word in the letter is addressed to the church's internal relations. Its themes are addressed to internal disputes and promoting peace within the church.

In the texts preceding Rom. 13:1–7, Paul exhorted everyone to live humbly according to the will of God (Rom. 12:1–2) and as part of a diverse body in Christ (Rom. 12:3–8), doing good to one another and returning evil with good (Rom. 12:9–21). In the texts following Rom. 13:1–7, Paul exhorted Christians to love one another as a fulfillment of the law (Rom. 13:8–10), improving in spirit (Rom. 13:11–14), and welcoming those who are weaker in faith instead of passing judgment on them (Rom. 14:1–23). These themes address relations within the context of the church.

Based on a superficial reading of what Paul said in Romans 12:14 about persecution, helping your enemy, and overcoming evil with good, there may be a temptation to see it as a discussion of relations with those outside the church, but it clearly isn't. The next verse placed that in context by referring to living in harmony with one another. This is a context of a young church that was immature because the members were hanging on to ways of thinking according to human wisdom, making enemies within the church. Its members were being factious, in fierce opposition to each other, and acting arrogantly toward and passing judgment on each other. The same sort of human wisdom that leads to oppression by those outside the church was creating oppression within the church. Therefore, the literary context offers no reason to believe that Paul was suddenly interjecting a different issue from internal relations for their consideration.

It would be more than a bit disjunctive and out of place to think that, in the midst of the other themes throughout the letter addressing internal church relations, Paul suddenly diverged for only seven short verses to talk briefly and vaguely about a complex theme of external relations with secular authorities, especially when interpreting it consistently with the subject of internal relations fits the context of the letter itself perfectly. Coherence of literary context suggests that Paul was talking about obedience to church authorities, not other types of authorities.

4. Theological coherence: Coherence of a primary theological theme of the letter suggests the same conclusion. If this text were read as addressing external relations to secular governments, it would have to be read as suddenly, and only for these few verses, reversing Paul's thematic emphasis on God's wisdom as replacing human wisdom. The text would then have to be read, out of context, as an injunction to follow blindly whatever human wisdom some secular government might require under the amazingly inconsistent argument that the authority was established by God. That illogical conclusion is theologically contrary to everything Paul said in his letter to the Romans. See, for example, Romans 1:18–23. Just one chapter earlier (Rom. 12:2), Paul urged the church not to be conformed to that world. Interpreting Romans 13:1–7 to require conformity he abhorred one chapter earlier is also theologically inconsistent with what Paul had said in any letter he had written.

The reference to the sword in Romans 13:4 is then a reference to the church's authority to discipline, including excommunicating those who would persist in causing dissension, a theme echoed in Romans 16:17. It is a metaphor used elsewhere in the New Testament for effecting important religious distinctions. Similar use of this sword imagery is found in Matthew 10:34–39: "Do not think that I have come to bring peace on earth; I have not come to bring peace but a sword. For I have come to set a man against his father." In support of that interpretation, compare the parallel passage in Luke 12:51–52, which speaks of that division but without the sword metaphor.

That sword is "not beat in vain" (Rom. 13:4) because it is not being used for vain human purposes, as secular governments would do. It is used instead by "a servant of God to execute his wrath on the wrongdoer." (Wrongdoer is defined by God's law, which secular governments don't know how to enforce, or have any direct interest in enforcing. See "Political context" below.) God's servant is obviously the church itself, distinct from other institutions that serve all manner of human wisdom.

Also, it is difficult to believe that Paul argued that obedience to God is designed to avoid the wrath of a vain and violent secular government such as Rome. Paul is clearly addressing obedience to the local church authority's efforts to maintain Christian community. The text cannot reasonably be suggesting that anyone look to the secular government to enforce God's laws. For example, Paul elsewhere chastises churches for bringing their internal disputes before secular authorities, effectively choosing to resolve their disputes according to the wisdom of men instead of the wisdom of God. See 1 Corinthians 6:1–6.

The reference in Romans 13:6–7 to taxes collected by authorities attending to God's ministry and respecting and honoring them is clearly not one to secular government that makes no effort to attend to God's ministry. The reference to taxes would have been understood, especially by Jewish Christians, to refer to the Jewish tithe or the tax for supporting the temple or possibly a similar Christian tax collected by the local Christian leaders patterned after a Jewish tax.

Recall that Paul himself was collecting money for the poor in Jerusalem, which he explained in Romans 15:25–28 and 1 Corinthians 16:1–4. According to the latter text, donations were expected from Christians who prospered. As such, it was like a tax because Christians who could afford to would naturally be expected to contribute according to their means. See also 2 Corinthians 8:1–9:15.

In addition to contributions for the poor in Jerusalem, Paul received contributions to support his own ministry to new churches. See 2 Corinthians 11:7–9. Paul clearly believed that Christians are obliged to do good by supporting the church as they can and that flows thematically into Romans 13:8: "Owe no one anything, except to love one another; for he who loves his neighbor has fulfilled the law."

5. Political context: Political context is well covered in the other categories, so the treatment here will be brief. Secular governments are established by humans for human political purposes pursuant to a human wisdom and promoting and enforcing that wisdom. They are not established to enforce God's wisdom, and any such enforcement would require the secular government to abandon its own wisdom, strategies, and structures.

God might, of course, use secular governments for some special purpose, and there was some precedent for that view in the Old Testament. But to conclude that there is any broad and inclusive identity of purpose between God and any secular government generally is a terrible misunderstanding and a perverse rendering of Romans 13:1–7. In contrast, however, it is entirely consistent to think that there is (or ought to be) such a broad identity of purpose between God and church authorities.

6. New Testament theological context generally: Any view that secular institutions were established by God is clearly opposite to and irreconcilable with any other New Testament writing. For example, Ephesians 6:12 reads, "For we are not contending against flesh and blood, but against principalities, against the powers, against the world rulers of this present darkness, against the spiritual hosts of wickedness in the heavenly places."

Christians are therefore in opposition to principalities and world rulers instead of bound to obey them. The opposition to world rulers, of course, is not to them as people, for as people they are also part of God's creation to which good should be done. The opposition is instead religious or philosophical because they represent spiritual darkness (human wisdom). It doesn't make sense to think that Paul was arguing that Christians should be obedient to that spiritual darkness.

There are other New Testament texts that promoted peaceful relations with and encouraged praying for secular governments. That is in accord with Jesus' teaching to love our enemies and pray for them but it is not a blanket endorsement of their philosophies and activities. It is also consistent with diplomatic courtesy. For example, 1 Peter 2:12–17 advised Christians to honor human institutions and their officers to make their adherents think well of, instead of evil toward, Christians. See also, for example, 1 Timothy 2:1–4.

Paul also adopted analogous advice between the mature and the immature within the church for much the same reason that immature Christians continue in some respects think in a human way like those outside the church. In Romans 14, he advised the more mature not to act in a way to offend the immature: "So do not let your good be spoken of as evil" (Rom. 14:16).

Those goodwill purposes are hardly an assertion that there is a common purpose between God and secular authorities justifying submission and obedience to secular authorities as if obedience to them is somehow obedience to God. The texts of Ephesians and 1 Timothy cited above presume that kings and others in high positions don't yet know the truth. While the emperor is honored (as are all people), God is feared (1 Peter 2:17), which is to say that God is obeyed in the event of any conflict between them.

It is politically as well as theologically impossible to reconcile letting a secular government rule our life when we contend that

God rules our life. As Jesus said, one cannot serve two masters (Matt. 6:24). It is absurd to think that Paul was suggesting anything to the contrary, especially in the context of a letter urging immature Christians to abandon their human wisdom in favor of God's wisdom.

Interpreting Romans 13:1–7 to refer to secular government would make that text unique in the New Testament, contrary to Paul's own theology as well as that of the rest of New Testament. Governing authorities and rulers cannot reasonably be given a secular construction in Romans 13.

7. Historical context: Should Paul, by virtue of an interpretation of Romans 13:1–7 to refer to secular authority, be read to insist that Jesus was properly executed by the Romans acting under God's authority because Jesus was preaching about the kingdom of God instead of the kingdom of Rome? That would be nonsense. Every Christian who interprets Romans 13:1–7 like this would crucify Jesus again and again, stripping God's approval from Jesus and placing it on the likes of Nero, Hitler, and Stalin.

Such an interpretation is likewise historically inconsistent with the early church's persecution. While the probable dating of Paul's letter to the Roman church is before formal persecution of Christians began by the Roman Empire, that persecution began shortly thereafter. The letter is dated roughly 54–58 AD; persecutions by Rome began around 64 AD under Nero. Tradition is that Paul was eventually executed at the hands of Rome, perhaps even at Nero's direction, but hardly because Paul's conduct was offensive to God, as Romans 13:1–7 would suggest if given an interpretation that secular governments are established by God to do God's work.

In historical context, it is unlikely that early Christians would ever have cherished this text if it were a reference to secular government. It would have been a great offense to Paul and other early Christian martyrs, Jesus, and God if Romans 13:1–7 were understood to embrace and approve Roman persecution of Christians and Jesus. It would have been offensive to approve, by such an interpretation of this text, the Roman requirement that Christians bow down to Caesar as a god as if that Roman requirement were under God's authority.

In historical fact, Christians were persecuted by Rome because they remained loyal to God, refusing to worship the emperor of Rome as a god. They were persecuted because of their loyalty to God, not because of disloyalty as if Romans 13:1–7 had required obedience to secular authorities in order to be obedient to God. The letter and Paul would hardly have retained the prominence they did in the early church if that text were understood by early Christians to refer to secular government instead of church authorities.

Consideration of the entire context compels the conclusion that Romans 13:1–7 is intended as a reference to duly appointed church authorities, not to secular authorities. It was intended to do so to further unity and peace within the church, according to God's peace.

Romans 13:1–7 should not be confused with, for example, Matthew 22:15–22, where Jesus says, "Render therefore to Caesar the things that are Caesar's, and to God the things that are God's." The latter statement was also not a naive endorsement of whatever any government may demand. Instead, it recognized a distinction between things that belong to a human government vis-a-vis God's government. Jesus distinguished worldviews and their consequent systems—institutions that are man-made from those which are natural. The specific question put to Jesus was in regard to paying taxes to Caesar. Jesus' response effectively states that if one benefits financially from the artificial economy established by an artificial government, then by all means pay the taxes demanded by that government for its benefit. The statement reserves in no uncertain terms, however, everything that is part of the natural world to God's dominion, because those things are God's, in lieu of any competing claim of dominion by any artificial government over something it did not create.

Paul followed Romans 13:1–7 by repeating his theme that Christian love, doing good, fulfills God's law in Romans 13:8–10, and Christians need to become more mature in that love (Rom. 13:11–14).

Paul urged the church at Rome to put aside all reasons for despising one another, divisiveness, or judging one another. Instead, he wanted them to do what was good for fellow Christians. Those who are strong should bear with the weak (Rom. 15:1). In everything, they should do what is good for their neighbor (Rom. 15:2–3), seeking to live in harmony (Rom. 15:5), welcoming one another as they were welcomed into the church (Rom. 15:7).

Paul concluded with a statement of confidence that the Roman church was full of goodness and knowledge (Rom. 15:14). He acknowledged that he had talked to them boldly because of his own commitment as a minister of Christ Jesus (Rom. 15:15–16). His focus had been on working for God (Rom. 15:17) and for that reason his work also had been elsewhere rather than in Rome where others had been working to the same end, though he had longed to go to Rome (Rom. 15:18–23). Paul nevertheless expressed hope to visit Rome on his way to Spain after first going back to Jerusalem with contributions for the poor (Rom. 15:24–29).

Paul asked for their prayers (Rom. 15:30–32) and closed with a benediction that the God of peace be with them (Rom. 15:33).

Chapter 16 is primarily introductions and requests to greet Paul's fellow workers, except for one brief reminder to avoid dissensions (Rom. 16:17–20) and a final benediction.

Paul's letter to the Romans is overall a practical letter. It addresses practical issues faced by a new church of people from different backgrounds and walks of life. The practical lessons it offers can be applied today to any divisiveness within the church, which has its origin in human wisdom and artificial divisions, and to encourage focusing on the unifying and peaceful wisdom of God.